INDESCRIBABLE

ENCOUNTERING THE GLORY OF GOD
IN THE BEAUTY OF THE UNIVERSE

LOUIE GIGLIO
MATT REDMAN

David C Cook®

transforming lives together

IF THE STARS SHOULD
APPEAR ONE NIGHT IN A
THOUSAND YEARS, HOW MEN
WOULD BELIEVE AND ADORE.

—RALPH WALDO EMERSON

INDESCRIBABLE
Published by David C Cook
4050 Lee Vance View
Colorado Springs, CO 80918 U.S.A.

David C Cook Distribution Canada
55 Woodslee Avenue, Paris, Ontario, Canada N3L 3E5

David C Cook U.K., Kingsway Communications
Eastbourne, East Sussex BN23 6NT, England

The graphic circle C logo is a registered trademark of David C Cook.

The website addresses recommended throughout this book are offered as a resource to you.
These websites are not intended in any way to be or imply an endorsement on the part of
David C Cook, nor do we vouch for their content.

Unless otherwise noted, all Scripture quotations are taken from the Holy Bible, New
International Version®, NIV®. Copyright © 1973, 1978, 1984 by Biblica, Inc.™ Used by
permission of Zondervan. All rights reserved worldwide. www.zondervan.com. Scripture
quotations marked NLT are taken from the New Living Translation of the Holy Bible. New
Living Translation copyright © 1996, 2004 by Tyndale Charitable Trust. Used by permission
of Tyndale House Publishers. Scripture quotations marked ESV are taken from *The Holy Bible,
English Standard Version.* Copyright © 2000; 2001 by Crossway Bibles, a division of Good
News Publishers. Used by permission. All rights reserved.

The authors have added italics to Scripture quotations for emphasis.

LCCN 2011935866
ISBN 978-0-7814-0602-4
eISBN 978-1-4347-0458-0

© 2011 Louie Giglio and Matt Redman

The Team: Alex Field, Amy Konyndyk, Nick Lee, Renada Arens, Karen Athen
Cover Design: Leighton Ching
Cover Photo: Thierry Legault

Printed in the United States of America
First Edition 2011

1 2 3 4 5 6 7 8 9 10

082611

THIS BOOK IS DEDICATED TO OUR MOMS/MUMS,
LUMINOUS AND BEAUTIFUL: MARTHA JEANE GIGLIO
(IN LOVING MEMORY) AND BARBARA REDMAN.

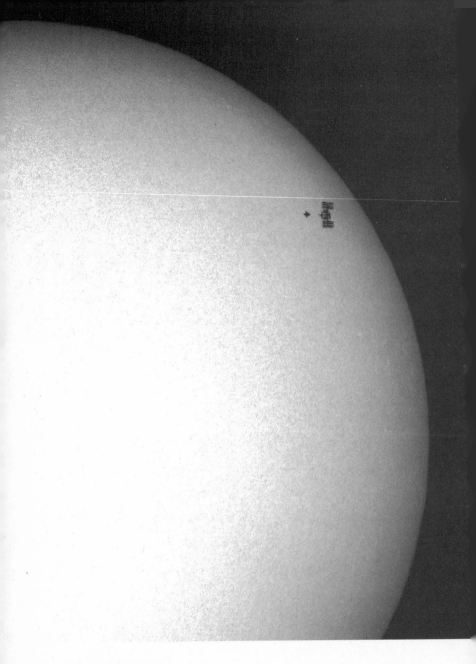

Cover Image (Close Up)
Solar transit of the space shuttle *Atlantis* (STS-132) less than one hour prior to docking with the
International Space Station (ISS), taken from Madrid, Spain, May 16, 2010. Aboard *Atlantis* were
copies of Matt's CD *We Shall Not Be Shaken* and Louie's DVD *How Great Is Our God*, carried into
space by Mission Specialist Michael T. Good.

Image: Thierry Legault

TABLE OF CONTENTS

FOREWORD BY FORMER ASTRONAUT JOE TANNER

"MECO, Atlantis"—the shuttle main engines have just shut down, and we are in orbit traveling 17,500 miles per hour. My goal of flying in space is finally realized after many years of preparation. Praise God! I look out a window to see Earth with my own eyes from 165 miles above its surface. It really is round! I feast on the beautiful colors below and then scan past the thin layer of our atmosphere to the vastness of space. The total blackness is pierced only by the brilliant rays of our Sun. I can't see any stars, only the emptiness of deep space. Is anything really out there?

My attention turns back to the sights below. Earth is beautiful beyond description. God must love us dearly to provide a planet so perfectly tuned for life in what appears to be an otherwise empty universe. As I enjoy the view and the comfort of His loving presence, I am convinced we serve an incredibly loving heavenly Father.

In only a few minutes, the scene changes while our spacecraft races around Earth. As the Sun slips rapidly below the horizon, I witness my first orbital sunset, further evidence of God's glory. With the growing darkness, I discover the emptiness is in fact filled with far more stars than I have ever seen or imagined. The majesty of this sight makes me aware that our planet is only a tiny speck in God's immense universe.

This first experience in space further convinced me that our God not only loves us; He is also unbelievably powerful to have created such a huge and magnificent universe. The only word that comes to mind is *indescribable!*

I am honored that Louie and Matt asked me to write a foreword to their book. The words and images in this book invite me to worship God, as did the space-flight views I just described. Allow Louie and Matt to take you on a journey to reveal God's love and glory in the universe.

May God richly bless you as you read.

JOE TANNER
Former NASA astronaut
STS-66, 82, 97, 115

FOREWORD BY ASTRONOMER JENNIFER WISEMAN

The book before you will lift your eyes to the skies, expand your mind, and refill your spirit with a new sense of the grandeur and awesome character of God.

When a friend recommended to me a few years ago that I watch the Louie Giglio video *Indescribable,* I smiled and thanked the well-meaning advocate, but I had little intention of actually watching it. Knowing that I am an astronomer myself, both a scientist and a follower of Jesus, my friend felt sure that I would be enamored with a presentation by a pastor that incorporated incredible discoveries of astronomy. But I had encountered quite a few disappointing religious presentations—books, films, sermons, and articles—in which the audience is left either with erroneous scientific claims, a sense that mainstream science is a foe of biblical faith, or both. How delighted I was to experience instead a passionate presentation of the awesomeness of God, exemplified by the incomprehensible magnitude and dynamic activity of the universe itself and elucidated with the latest scientific understanding.

Now in this book of the same name, Louie Giglio and Matt Redman build on the theme by sharing powerful observations of how the heavens have infused their own relationships with God with a sense of awe and joy. The heavens have also always inspired in me a sense of amazement and a desire to explore. I can't help but believe that a Creator responsible for countless wonders must take delight as we find out more and more of what's out there and how nature unfolds. Indeed, the advancements in telescope technology are allowing us to glimpse wonders that were only imagined just a few decades ago: merging galaxies, light-distorting dark matter, extrasolar planets, and even ancient light from near the dawn of the universe. Our discoveries tell us something about the nature of God as we see evidence of patience, beauty, incredible magnitude, and a flourishing of life—at least on one planet!

May you be inspired to take the time to "look up," both with your own eyes and through the incredible images now available online from the world's most powerful telescopes. And may the thoughts shared in this book help you to make connections between the God of an awesome universe and the love He has for you and this tiny, beautiful planet.

JENNIFER WISEMAN
Astronomer, author, and speaker

Sombrero Galaxy
The Sombrero Galaxy has been observed and wondered at for centuries. Also known as M104 or NGC 4594, the Sombrero Galaxy is an unbarred spiral galaxy located twenty-nine million light-years from Earth in the constellation Virgo.

Image: NASA and the Hubble Heritage Team (STScI/AURA)

BEGINNINGS

Matt and I both consider ourselves lead worshippers, those called to lead people into God's presence, helping give voice to generations as they echo His splendor in worship. While Matt most often leads through the medium of music, writing songs that have shaped how the church worships around the world, my role has more often been that of preacher. Yet, in each case, our desire is to paint as big a picture of God as we possibly can, expanding people's concept of His greatness and glory.

Somewhere along the journey, we discovered we share an appreciation for the universe that surrounds us, particularly its unique ability to lift our hearts to see how massive and mysterious God truly is. With beauty and wonder, the heavens affirm that the One who spoke them into existence is more amazing than we have imagined, something Matt and I have attempted to reflect in our music and speaking.

As Paul Hawken keenly observed,

> Ralph Waldo Emerson once asked what we would
> do if the stars only came out once every thousand
> years. No one would sleep that night, of course....
> We would be ecstatic, delirious, made rapturous
> by the glory of God. Instead, the stars come out
> every night and we watch television.[1]

It's true the stars can be ignored. But it's also true that they can lead us to wonder … and to their Maker.

Matt and I share a love for books about the cosmos, especially the image-rich variety that allow us the chance to get up close and personal with the universe. So it's not surprising that in time, a dream was hatched to compile a book of both images and text, a devotional journey that points us back to the Creator.

It's our desire that *Indescribable* will do just that, and that believer and seeker alike will be ushered into a deeper understanding of the One who fashioned not just a world but our hearts as well.

LOUIE AND MATT

NOTES:
1 Paul Hawken, "Commencement Address to the Class of 2009, University of Portland, May 3, 2009," www.commondreams.org/view/2009/05/23-2.

Infrared View of Orion Nebula
Image: ESO/J. Emerson/VISTA. Acknowledgment: Cambridge Astronomical Survey Unit

LOST IN WONDER

WE ARE SURROUNDED BY A GRAND AND GLORIOUS COSMOS, HEAVENS BEYOND OUR COMPREHENSION.

Just how big we do not know, but we do know that even in light of humanity's great inventions, the stars have a way of drowning out our fuss—reducing our earthly clatter with their sheer immensity all while heightening a sense of mystery and wonder within our souls. You don't have to be an astronomer or have any scientific interest to be suddenly swept away by their vastness and beauty. All you have to do is look up.

Night after night, hosts of shimmering stars stretch our ability to comprehend their expanse. And at times, they literally take our breath away. For me, one of those times came on a winter night in Juneau, Alaska, when a phenomenon known as the northern lights roared into town in all its glory.

As we sat in a brightly lit mall restaurant, even the locals were stunned when we saw brilliant greenish lights dancing in the sky.

In an instant, we jumped up from the table and bolted for the car. We drove until we were beyond the reach of city lights, stopping at a place near the airport runway where pitch-black night enveloped us below and something difficult to describe in words hovered above.

It looked as if a superluminous LED screen had replaced the sky, projecting bold blasts of neon green across the black backdrop, brilliant colors shifting this way and that way in the blink of an eye. Random patterns and streaks of light whizzed above me, moving like nothing I had ever seen or imagined. To be honest, at first I was a little afraid, then speechless, but soon I started running and screaming at the top of my lungs.

When I finally made it back to my hotel, my heart was still beating so hard that I called my wife, Shelley, waking her up in the middle of the night. Yet I was unable to fully convey what I had just seen and experienced.

I remember another night, sleeping alongside the Colorado River at the bottom of the Grand Canyon, a mile-deep crevice in the Arizona dirt, where the darkest darkness made the stars so close I kept reaching out in awe to touch them, though I knew they were millions of miles away.

And I will never forget my sister's birthday in 1969, as our family huddled late in the night around our black-and-white console television anxiously watching as Neil Armstrong set foot on the surface of the Moon, stunning the world. It was somewhere around midnight, and the sky over suburban Atlanta was mostly clear as I walked out of our sliding-glass door and gazed in absolute wonder at the glowing ball of white that hung overhead. I'd seen it a thousand times before, but on this night, my mind could barely take it in as I kept repeating to myself, "There are people up there … right now. There are people just like me walking on the Moon."

THE SIGNIFICANCE AND JOY IN MY SCIENCE COMES IN THOSE OCCASIONAL MOMENTS OF DISCOVERING SOMETHING NEW AND SAYING TO MYSELF, "SO THAT'S HOW GOD DID IT."

—HENRY "FRITZ" SCHAEFER
GRAHAM PERDUE PROFESSOR OF CHEMISTRY AND DIRECTOR OF THE CENTER FOR COMPUTATIONAL QUANTUM CHEMISTRY AT THE UNIVERSITY OF GEORGIA

If you're old enough to remember that night, you know the feeling I'm talking about. But at some point *all* of us have leaned our heads back in amazement as we've tried to compute the starry host that surrounds us. A sense of smallness and awe invades our hearts while in reverent wonder we consider the expanse of the universe and our tiny estate. The feeling is that of *falling up*, the humility that settles on the soul when we consider the immensity of the world in which we live.

Matt and I are so glad you've picked up this book and have started to read, especially knowing that this cosmos stuff wows each of us to varying degrees. While we can all appreciate the beauty of the heavens, not everyone has the same threshold for the facts and figures of astronomy.

This was underscored for me a few years ago as Shelley and I were enjoying a stress-free afternoon under the Caribbean Sun. Clinging lazily to the float we shared as we bobbed in pristine waters, I couldn't help but notice the Sun sinking toward Earth's horizon as it finished its course for the day.

The night before I had dived headlong into a book about the many variables needed to sustain life on Earth—or on any planet. Looking up at the late-day Sun, I sat stunned by what I had discovered about the unique Earth-Sun-Moon relationship, which allows us to happily exist on our planet home and to observe the universe around us from the best vantage point possible.

Since Shelley and I weren't talking about anything in particular, I began to share some of the facts I had learned. For example: Both the Sun and the Moon appear the same size in Earth's sky because though the Sun is four hundred times larger than the Moon, it is also four hundred times farther away.[1] Amazing. And this fact: The Moon is the perfect size to contribute to a habitable Earth. If the Moon were larger, it would cause Earth to tilt so far on its axis that the side facing the Sun would experience unbearable heat while the opposite side of Earth would know perpetual subzero winter. As it is, the Moon is just the right size to cause Earth to tilt at a very acceptable 23.4 degrees, bringing both winter and summer to the planet.[2] A larger Moon would also slow Earth's rotation greatly (Earth is now slowing at a rate of 1.4 milliseconds a day per century[3]), lengthening the day and creating a hostile climate.

I was just beginning to tell Shelley about the importance of the Moon's gravitational pull—which helps create upper-level winds that aid in the distribution of rain throughout Earth—when Shelley interjected with a very serious look, asking, "And what year did scientists discover the Moon is made of cheese?" and totally cracked herself up. I kept a straight face as long as I could, but eventually succumbed to the irony of it all as we both laughed out loud.

Fair enough. Each of us have a different approach to science, and in this case, astronomy (not unlike our varying tastes in music, finance, fashion, sports, and the like). But everyone, everywhere, at some point in life, has gazed into the night sky and felt a sense of wonder. That's what this book is all about. Matt and I filled these pages with descriptions and images that overwhelm our senses and strain our comprehension. But they also do far more, stirring something inside the soul, beckoning us to something greater, Someone more. Socrates wrote, "Philosophy begins in wonder."[4] I think it's true that worship begins in wonder as well.

Columbia Moonrise
Taken on January 26, 2003, by the crew of the space shuttle *Columbia*, this image reveals a quarter Moon viewed over Earth's horizon. Six days later, the crew of the *Columbia* was tragically killed when the shuttle broke up on its return trip to Earth.

Image: NASA

The glorious darkness that so accentuates the lights of heaven lifts us upward and draws us into its chorus. The longer we look up, the freer we become, lost in the wonder and mystery that surround us, lost in praise of the One who set each star in place. Broken humanity has a ferocious gravitational pull, constantly shrinking us down to Earth. But as we lift our gaze to the skies, how can we not know in our hearts that there must be more?

> *The heavens are telling the glory of God, their expanse declares the work of His hands. Day after day they pour forth speech, and night after night they tell us what they know. There is no place where there is speech where their voices are not heard. (Psalm 19:1–3, author's paraphrase)*

Looking up makes us feel small and shrouds us with a sense of awe, but that's never a bad thing. So let that feeling come (and stay) as you journey through these pages. And let the wonder of it all lift you up to see and embrace the face of God, the brilliant Maker of all.

LG

NOTES:

1. Iain Nicolson, *Unfolding Our Universe* (New York: Cambridge University Press, 1999), 2.
2. Ken Croswell, *Magnificent Mars* (New York: Free Press, 2003), 88.
3. Martin Ince, *The Rough Guide to the Earth* (London: Rough Guides Ltd., 2007), 40.
4. Socrates, quoted in Ryan K. Balot, ed., *A Companion to Greek and Roman Political Thought* (West Sussex, UK: Blackwell, 2009), 326.

*ASTRONOMY COMPELS THE
SOUL TO LOOK UPWARDS.*

—PLATO

Spiral Galaxy NGC 1232
This spectacular image of the large spiral galaxy NGC 1232 is based on three exposures in ultra-violet, blue, and red light, respectively. NGC 1232 is located in the constellation Eridanus, about one hundred million light-years from Earth, but the excellent optical quality of the VLT and FORS allows us to see an incredible wealth of detail. NGC 1232 spans two hundred thousand light-years, or about twice the size of the Milky Way Galaxy.

CH 2 // MATT REDMAN
MANY KINDS OF SPLENDOR

WHEN IT COMES TO LOOKING AT THE STARS, YOU AND I LIVE IN A PRIVILEGED AGE. A FEW HUNDRED YEARS AGO, astronomers believed there to be only around six thousand stars out there in the universe. But in more recent times, these figures have been blown right out of the water—and we've come to realize just how short their estimations fell. Astronomers now believe there to be more stars in the visible universe (what we know to be there) than there are grains of sand on all of the world's beaches and deserts.[1] As it turns out, we're even smaller than we thought we were. And our Creator God is far mightier than we ever imagined Him to be.

But the show is by no means over. Every cosmic discovery scientists make today underlines just how much is still to be seen. The newest evidence suggests that there are somewhere between one hundred and two hundred billion galaxies in the universe, each of them containing hundreds of billions of stars.[2] And as most scientists agree, there still seems to be no end in sight.

BY INVESTIGATING GOD'S MAJESTIC AND AWESOME CREATION, SCIENCE CAN ACTUALLY BE A MEANS OF WORSHIP.

—FRANCIS COLLINS
*DIRECTOR, NATIONAL INSTITUTES OF HEALTH
FORMER DIRECTOR OF THE HUMAN GENOME PROJECT*

The last twenty years have ushered us into the most privileged age of all. In April 1990 the Hubble Space Telescope was unveiled, and with it a whole new era of seeing the wonders of God's handiwork. Not only has this telescope allowed us to see farther, but it has helped us see the majesty of these celestial creations in far greater detail.

In its orbit above the distorting effects of Earth's atmosphere, Hubble is allowing us to gaze upon some of the most awe-inspiring sights ever known to humanity. As one astronomer commented, "Literally every place [the Hubble Space Telescope] has looked, it has found something fantastic."[3] Making one splendor-filled discovery after another, this instrument is turning out to be one of the world's best worship leaders, introducing us to scenes of such compelling majesty that to bow low before our Maker is the only fitting response.

In 1 Corinthians we read, "The sun has one kind of splendor, the moon another and the stars another; and star differs from star in splendor" (15:41).

When we look up and begin to search out the wonders of the heavens, we find many kinds of splendor. We see countless stars like our Sun, burning violently in a process of nuclear fusion. We encounter supernovas—massive stars in the throes of death—blazing even more extravagantly. During their final stages, these dying stars can shine brighter than an entire galaxy. We find neutron stars— so compacted and dense that scientists predict one teaspoon worth would weigh a billion tons.[4] Spinning around at speeds of up to six hundred revolutions per second, these stars are far beyond our imagining.[5] We also find collections of stars—clusters and galaxies with hundreds, thousands, and billions of stars in beautiful formations. We discover other objects too, such as nebulae—stunning clouds of gas and dust, far larger than we could ever fathom.

Yes, when we survey the expanse of the universe, we encounter so many kinds of splendor. Throughout this book we'll journey through several of them, witnessing the beauty and the power of these inspiring creations. Along the way we pray you will find yourself caught up in the wonders of the God they reflect.

In the biblical account of the birth of Jesus, it was a star that led the wise men to find Him. But God had been using stars to point people to Himself long before this momentous event. Yes, the heavens declare the glory of God—and Louie and I hope that this book will lead you to do the same.

MR

NOTES:
1. Mark Richard Kidger, *Cosmological Enigmas: Pulsars, Quasars, and Other Deep-Space Questions* (Baltimore: Johns Hopkins University Press, 2007), 144.
2. Fraser Cain, "How Many Galaxies in the Universe?" *Universe Today,* May 4, 2009, www.universetoday.com/30305/how-many-galaxies-in-the-universe.
3. Mario Livio, quoted in Sharon Begley, "When Galaxies Collide," *Newsweek,* November 3, 1997, 33.
4. Neil F. Comins, *Discovering the Essential Universe* (New York: W. H. Freeman, 2009), 232.
5. Max Camenzind, *Compact Objects in Astrophysics: White Dwarfs, Neutron Stars, and Black Holes* (Berlin: Springer, 2007), 270.

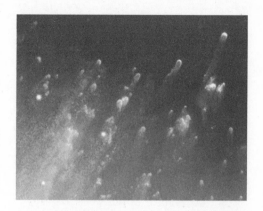

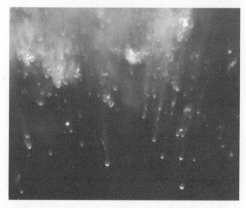

Helix Nebula (close-up)
Images: NASA, NOAO, ESA, the
Hubble Helix Team, M. Meixner
(STScI), and T. A. Rector (NRAO)

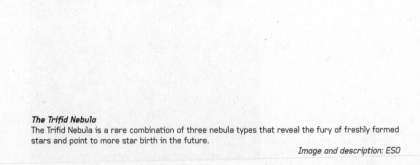

The Trifid Nebula
The Trifid Nebula is a rare combination of three nebula types that reveal the fury of freshly formed stars and point to more star birth in the future.

Image and description: ESO

CH 3 // MATT REDMAN
INDESCRIBABLE

EVEN WHEN IT COMES TO RELAXING, I'M A MAN WHO LIKES TO MULTITASK. SO, RECENTLY I FOUND MYSELF watching a music-awards show on TV, while at the same time reading a book on outer space. It wasn't too long before the bizarre contrast started to hit me. The fleeting and momentary applause lavished on the award winners compared with the enduring applause of the starry night sky lavished on the God of all creation. The brief and earthly "and the winner is …" announcements of the ceremony versus the continuing nuclear-fused declarations of the heavens, radiating out for millions of miles around.

Throughout the evening, the announcements became bolder and bolder: "And now welcome to the stage the multimillion-selling, the one and only global superstar …!" Yet, however hard the award presenters searched for words, they just couldn't compete with these fiery creations exploding off the pages of the book I was reading, announcing the glory of the true One and Only.

THE VERY ORDER, DISPOSITION, BEAUTY, CHANGE AND MOTION OF THE WORLD AND OF ALL VISIBLE THINGS SILENTLY PROCLAIM THAT IT COULD ONLY HAVE BEEN MADE BY GOD.

—AUGUSTINE

The point is this: These incomparable and unfathomable wonders above tell us of a God who is quite simply ... *indescribable*.

> Indescribable, uncontainable
> You placed the stars in the sky and You know them
>   by name;
> You are amazing, God.[1]

On a clear night, from the best standpoints on Earth, it's possible for the human eye to see around two thousand stars—an impressive and inspiring sight. Yet through the eyes of modern science, we're realizing just how much more there is to see out there. Though ultimately we have no way of knowing, astronomers now estimate there to be around 70,000 million million million stars in the visible universe alone.[2] And who knows how many more may be out there, beyond our current explorations and estimations? In the book of Genesis, God spoke to Abraham and said, "Look up at the heavens and count the stars—if indeed you can count them" (15:5). This very same challenge, issued thousands of years ago, still stands strong today. For who can number the stars in this vast and expanding universe?

Astronomers are encountering objects heavier, denser, hotter, and brighter than our human minds can ever begin to comprehend. The biggest and brightest known star in our own galaxy is Eta Carinae, part of the Carina Nebula, NGC 3372 (also known as the Keyhole Nebula). The extreme brightness of this object, which is more than one hundred times more massive than the Sun, is attributed to the fact it's a star in the throes of death—exploding violently in a blaze of dust and gas during its final stages. As Werner Gitt writes,

> If the sun and Eta Carinae were at the same distance from the earth, [Eta Carinae] would be 4 million times as bright as the sun.[3]

But even this is not the brightest object out there. During its final stages, a supernova (a form of dying star) may shine brighter than the whole galaxy in which it's placed. Take, for example, Supernova 1987A, which during the peak of its luminosity was thought to be shining over one hundred million times brighter than the Sun![4] These figures are completely off the charts, once again filling us with reverence and awe for our indescribable Maker. He simply spoke … and there they were.

The sheer size of stars can also floor us. Scientists have located a huge star called IRS 65. To demonstrate just how massive it is, they say that if our Sun were only eighteen inches high, then in comparison IRS 65 would stand as tall as Mount Everest.[5]

Next up are neutron stars. Talk about the wow factor. Some astronomers estimate that neutron stars may actually be ten trillion times denser than steel.[6] But it's not only their density that dazzles us—it's their frantic activity, too. Some neutron stars spin at rates of up to six hundred times per second.[7] It seems that Annie Dillard was right when she looked up and concluded, "The Creator loves pizzazz."[8]

So often we'll view the wonders God has made and comment on His incredible creativity. And so we should—for we see colors,

Centaurus A
Image of Centaurus A, revealing the lobes and jets emanating from the active galaxy's central black hole.

Image and description: ESO/WFI (Optical); MPIfR/ESO/APEX/A. Weiss et al. (Submillimetre); NASA/CXC/CfA/R. Kraft et al. (X-ray)

patterns, and order too beautiful for words. But through all that He has made, God is not just displaying the wonderful heights of His creative prowess. He is also showing us His mighty strength. These stars in all their furious and explosive glory convey the unrivaled power of a mighty Creator. In the book of Isaiah, for example, God keeps pointing us to the cosmos as a reminder of His great and unmatchable strength:

> *I am the LORD, who has made all things, who alone stretched out the heavens. (44:24)*

> *My own hands stretched out the heavens; I marshaled their starry hosts. (45:12)*

He alone is God, and no one else is even near qualified for the job. But in case we need to check references, or examine His résumé, He stuns us with His creation. The book of Job drives the point home:

> *And these are but the outer fringe of his works; how faint the whisper we hear of him! Who then can understand the thunder of his power? (26:14)*

For as awe-inspiring as they are, even these nuclear-fueled stars and spiraled galaxies are not the heights of God's power. They are inutterably grand and overwhelmingly impressive. And yet even these are not the whole picture. They are not His *pièce de résistance* or the limits of His ability. Instead, they are tiny echoes of the might of who He really is. The faintest whispers of His thunderous power and strength. Who then can comprehend the full heights of His majesty?

Perhaps one of the most striking things is not all that we *can* see—but all that we *can't*. As we peer farther and farther into the reaches of the universe, our exploration has gone only to affirm that there's far more out there than we will ever know. The more we discover, the more it becomes apparent that in His divine extravagance, God made "extra."

But why create stretches of the universe that will never be seen? Why be content for distant galaxies to go completely unnoticed for thousands and thousands of years? It is a mark of extravagance in the heart of our Creator God. God is not like us. So often our nature is to cut corners. If there's a room people rarely go into, we're unlikely to consider keeping it tidy. Or say, for example, we're decorating a room, and there's a piece of wall hidden from sight. We may not go to the trouble of painting it. Yet the Maker of all things is not like that. He does not cut corners or sweep things under the carpet. He has stretched out the universe, creating beauty in places our eyes—and even our telescopes—will likely never have the privilege of gazing upon. He is a God of extravagance—unimaginably glorious, completely off the charts of our understanding, and way beyond the powers of our description.

If God is indescribable, where does that leave us? It leaves us walking more humbly than we've ever walked before—bowed at the thought of such a mighty and mysterious God. It leaves us safe in the knowledge of His ultimate control—that the One who spoke these awe-inspiring, inconceivable wonders into being will never lose

the plot or drop the ball. And it leaves us pondering just how much He—this creative God of hidden wonders—has in store for those who've chosen to love and follow Him.

MR

NOTES:

1. Laura Story, "Indescribable," *Indescribable,* 2002, compact disc.
2. "Star Survey Reaches 70 Sextillion," *CNN,* July 23, 2003, articles.cnn.com/2003-07-22/tech/stars. survey_1_sextillion-big-number-universe?_s=PM:TECH.
3. Werner Gitt, *Stars and Their Purpose: Understanding the Origin of Earth's "Nightlights"* (Green Forest, AZ: Master Books, 2006), 31.
4. Nigel Henbest and Heather Couper, *The Guide to the Galaxy* (New York: Cambridge University Press, 1994), 39.
5. Ken Boa (talk, Crossroads Church, Portland, OR, July 2004).
6. "Hubble Sees Bare Neutron Star Streaking Across Space," *HubbleSite,* November 9, 2000, hubblesite.org/newscenter/archive/releases/star/neutron%20 star/2000/35/text.
7. Lori Stiles, "Scientists Glimpse Exotic Matter in a Neutron Star," *UANews,* September 3, 2004, www.uanews.org/node/10042.
8. Annie Dillard, "Pilgrim at Tinker Creek," in *Three by Annie Dillard: Pilgrim at Tinker Creek, An American Childhood, The Writing Life* (New York: Harper Perennial, 1990), 135.

Pleiades

The Pleiades, or Seven Sisters, lie in the constellation Taurus, roughly 440 light-years from Earth. Shown here in an image taken by the Palomar 48-inch Schmidt telescope, the cluster is composed of about 1,000 stars. Some of the dust that helped give birth to these stars still remains, and reflects a bluish hue to Earth.

Image and description: NASA, ESA, AURA/Caltech, and STScI

CH 4 // LOUIE GIGLIO

SIGNIFICANT INSIGNIFICANCE

*BEHOLD A UNIVERSE
SO IMMENSE THAT I AM
LOST IN IT. I NO LONGER
KNOW WHERE I AM.
I AM JUST NOTHING AT ALL.
OUR WORLD IS TERRIFYING
IN ITS INSIGNIFICANCE.*

—BERNARD DE FONTENELLE

WHILE SCIENTISTS AREN'T ENTIRELY SURE JUST HOW BIG THE UNIVERSE IS, ONE THING IS CLEAR: WE ARE really small within it. In fact, in terms of scale, Earth itself is inconsequential amid the expanse of space around us. The same could be said for our entire solar system, and the Milky Way Galaxy, both of which, when it comes to size, really don't matter at all in the grand scheme of things.

Our entire solar system is tiny in the midst of the vast Milky Way, which itself is only one of billions of other galaxies in the known universe. By way of example, scientists say the size of our solar system relative to the Milky Way would be roughly the size of a quarter in an area as big as all of North America.[1] Imagine placing a quarter in your backyard, gaining enough altitude to view the entire North American continent at once, and then trying to find that quarter. No way. You wouldn't even be able to see your city or town.

Maybe, just maybe, we're not that big after all. But it's not for lack of trying, is it? In the early days, people tried to build a tower that would reach the heavens. Talk about self-confidence. And, in every generation since, we have worked to elevate our names and build things as if we could really garner fame that lasts. Yet the scope of the night sky seems to always have its way with us, and if we look too long, we will soon feel that shrinking feeling that Hermann Hagedorn so perceptively describes in "Starry Night."

> When the stars come out we are such little men
> That we must arm ourselves in glare and thunder,
> Or cave in on our own dry littleness.[2]

That's the way I felt the first time I saw the image that stunned the astronomical world. Mind you, at first glance, this picture looks like one of those "oops, my camera accidently went off in the bottom of my bag" photos.

It was February 14, 1990, and the *Voyager 1* spacecraft screamed through the darkness of space, traveling forty thousand miles per hour away from the Sun. Launched thirteen years earlier, in 1977, *Voyager* was now beyond Pluto, having successfully accomplished its mission of photographing each of our distant neighbor planets. Amazingly, though the spacecraft was flying past the edges of our solar system, scientists had *Voyager* take one last Earth-facing image before continuing on its one-way journey away from the Sun through space.

Spanning the canopy of black, *Voyager* snapped a series of 60 images, storing them for future delivery to Earth. Each of these 60 images consisted of 640,000 pixels (a pixel is one of the tiny series of dots that make up a photograph), yet because *Voyager* was

Pale Blue Dot
This famous image, dubbed the "Pale Blue Dot," is the first-ever external picture of our own solar system. Taken by the *Voyager* spacecraft, the image was compiled from 60 smaller photos taken in sequence. The bands of light are artifacts, resulting from sunlight and magnification. As an interesting coincidence, Earth lies inside one of the scattered Sun rays, comprising an area of only 0.12 pixels in the massive surrounding expanse.

Image: NASA Jet Propulsion Laboratory (NASA-JPL)

SUDDENLY, FROM BEHIND THE RIM OF THE MOON, IN LONG, SLOW-MOTION MOMENTS OF IMMENSE MAJESTY, THERE EMERGES A SPARKLING BLUE AND WHITE JEWEL, A LIGHT, DELICATE SKY-BLUE SPHERE LACED WITH SLOWLY SWIRLING VEILS OF WHITE, RISING GRADUALLY LIKE A SMALL PEARL IN A THICK SEA OF BLACK MYSTERY. IT TAKES MORE THAN A MOMENT TO FULLY REALIZE THIS IS EARTH ... HOME.

—EDGAR MITCHELL
APOLLO ASTRONAUT

now an estimated 3.7 billion miles from home, it took each individual pixel 5½ hours to make the journey back to Earth. Not 5½ hours for each photo, mind you, but 5½ hours for each of the 640,000 tiny dots in each picture.[3] Talk about waiting a long time for something to download! But finally, an image appeared. Dubbed "The Pale Blue Dot," the composite photograph captured within one of the colored shafts a tiny dot, scarcely visible to the naked eye. Yep, you guessed it. That little speck is Earth, photographed from almost 4 billion miles away.

Looking at the image, it's easy to see why it rocked the scientific community and everyone else who saw it. Not because we hadn't ever seen our planet before, but because we hadn't dreamed of seeing ourselves from this far away.

At the time, we had grown accustomed to seeing images of Earth from high above, mostly thanks to a multitude of groundbreaking photos from the Apollo missions. Those early glimpses of swirling clouds, greenish-brown lands, and deep blue seas caused us to stop and consider just how small we truly are. But with this image, we found ourselves looking back at Earth from beyond the edge of our own solar system. And what do we see? No land or sea. No continents or nations. No mountain peaks or towering cities. No evidence of life, or humanity, or any earthly thing. Certainly, we can't see you or me.

Reflecting on the image, Carl Sagan, the most famed astronomer of the day, noted:

> That's here. That's home. That's us. On it every-
> one you love, everyone you know, everyone you

ever heard of, every human being who ever was, lived out their lives. The aggregate of our joy and suffering, thousands of confident religions, ideologies, and economic doctrines, every hunter and forager, every hero and coward, every creator and destroyer of civilization, every king and peasant, every young couple in love, every mother and father, hopeful child, inventor and explorer, every teacher of morals, every corrupt politician, every "superstar," every "supreme leader," every saint and sinner in the history of our species lived there—on a mote of dust suspended in a sunbeam.

The Earth is a very small stage in a vast cosmic arena.... Our posturings, our imagined self-importance, the delusion that we have some privileged position in the Universe, are challenged by this point of pale light.[4]

I couldn't agree more. The image confirms what the ancient Scriptures say about us: that we are so much smaller than we think. We are tiny. Frail. Minute. We are vapors inhabiting a miniscule speck in a measureless sea of cosmic wonder. Looking up into the dark night sky, the same feeling must have washed over the psalmist as he wrote, "When I consider your heavens, the work of your fingers, the moon and the stars, which you have set in place, what is man that you are mindful of him, the son of man that you care for him?" (Ps. 8:3–4).

Spiral Galaxy NGC 628
Made up of about one hundred billion stars, NGC 628 sits face-on to Earth about thirty million light-years away. The galaxy has many similarities to our own and is a striking example of symmetry and detail.

Image: NASA, ESA, and the Hubble Heritage (STScI/AURA)-ESA/Hubble Collaboration
Acknowledgment: R. Chandar (University of Toledo) and J. Miller (University of Michigan)

This sentiment was echoed by Neil Armstrong when he said, "I remember on the trip home on Apollo 11 it suddenly struck me that that tiny pea, pretty and blue, was the earth. I put up my thumb and shut one eye, and my thumb blotted out the planet earth. I didn't feel like a giant. I felt very, very small."[5]

There is a certain sense of lostness that invades our hearts when we look up into the skies above or look back at ourselves from billions of miles in space. But are we merely nothing, an infinitesimal people living out our meaningless days on a tiny blue speck? There's no doubting that we're small (really, really small), but are we intrinsically insignificant?

Apparently Sagan thought so. He concludes this way:

> Our planet is a lonely speck in the great enveloping cosmic dark. In our obscurity, in all this vastness, there is no hint that help will come from elsewhere to save us from ourselves.[6]

It's at this point that Sagan and I part ways.

As for the "hint" Sagan speaks of, I would invite you to look more closely at the little speck suspended in the beam of light. If you look closely enough at the pale blue dot, you'll find, beside a busy roadway, just outside a small city, on a hot and searing afternoon thousands of years ago, a cross that still looms ever so large in history and eternity. On this cross hung not just one of us, but God Himself in human flesh—the originator of the vast universe who engulfs us by giving His life for us all. His name? Jesus—the name itself meaning He would *save His people from their sins.* For love Jesus chose to come to this "mote of dust," embodying God's indelible proclamation: "I love you." How amazing that, on this tiny cosmic speck, His incomprehensible death provided a covering for our fall-enness, His resurrection life bridging the way back to the arms of our Maker.

Looking back across time at this little sphere that we call home, I cannot escape the feeling that comes over me. Yet, looking at the wonder of the cross of Christ, I can't help but see God's irrepressible stamp of significance on tiny, insignificant people like you and me.

LG

NOTES:

1. Bruce McClure, "Where Is the Ecliptic in Relation to the Milky Way?" *EarthSky,* January 22, 2008, earthsky.org/space/where-is-the-ecliptic-in-relation-to-the-milky-way.
2. Hermann Hagedorn, "Starry Night," in James Dalton Morrison, ed., *Masterpieces of Religious Verse* (New York: Harper, 1948), 28.
3. Carl Sagan, *The Pale Blue Dot* (New York: Random House, 1994), 2.
4. Ibid., 6–7.
5. Neil Armstrong, quoted in James L. Christian, *Philosophy: An Introduction to the Art of Wondering* (Belmont, CA: Wadsworth Cengage Learning, 2009), 373.
6. Sagan, 7.

Lunar Transit
This transit of the Moon across the Sun on February 25, 2007, was visible only from the STEREO-B spacecraft in its orbit about the Sun, trailing behind Earth.

The Sun as it appears here is a composite of images in four different wavelengths of extreme ultraviolet light that were separated into color channels and then recombined.

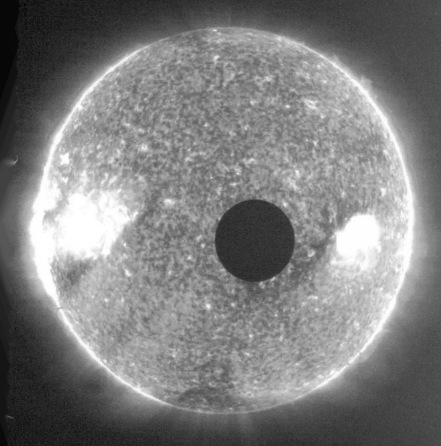

STOP AND CONSIDER

ON A RECENT EVENING I RETURNED HOME AFTER A FRANTIC DAY OF MEETINGS. STEPPING OUT OF THE CAR, I looked up to the starry sky above, amazed at what a clear night it was. And I stood there in wonder.

For all of thirty seconds.

Something else had grabbed my attention. Another celestial wonder perhaps? A shooting star? No, something mundane and miniscule. Catching a glimpse of the TV through the front window of the house, I noticed that my favorite show was starting. I hurried inside and headed right for the couch. An hour or two later, the absurdity and ignorance of what I'd done dawned on me. I'd traded in the sight of something truly extraordinary and potentially soul inspiring to engage in something ordinary and far less edifying. I'd refused the opportunity to "stop"—to pause for a little longer under that beautiful display of the heavens and encounter the glory of God in the beauty of His universe.

Here we stand in an age that is thirsting for wonder. In our information-overloaded society, there seems to be no room left for mystery and fascination. Yet just when we're tempted to shrink God down to size—or kick Him out of the equation altogether—there in front of our eyes stand the wonders of His universe. A great big, awe-inspiring reminder of just who it is we're dealing with.

Worship has no room for "know-it-alls." The soul who lives in the ordinary and the mundane will rarely aspire to climb higher in praise. And reverence for God will never flow freely from a heart that shrinks Him down to earthly proportions. God makes worshippers out of wonderers. If we will allow them, the beauty and vastness of the cosmos will help lead us to higher ground in worship.

As we read in the book of Job, "Stop and consider God's wonders" (37:14). The first stage is simply to "stop." You cannot begin to consider if you do not first stop. Reverence is often the fruit of reflection, and reflection often the result of stillness. But in our task-driven culture, so many of us have forgotten where the pause button is. Our society doesn't encourage reflection, and we have much to learn from the many streams of the church that throughout history have put a strong emphasis on slowing down to listen, meditate, and wonder. Jesus Himself, as He walked Earth, set aside important time to pause and pray, finding stillness away from all the noise. Once we learn to stop, we soon begin to consider. If we will lift our eyes and look up, the beauty and power of the cosmos will amaze us into worship. We begin to count the stars, considering just how incredible it is that each and every one is far brighter, hotter, and larger than we could ever begin to imagine. We strain our eyes upward, wondering just how far away they must be, and just how long their light must have taken to travel to us. We realize that there is nothing human hands could ever create that comes remotely near the magnitude and

THE UNIVERSE IS FULL OF MAGICAL THINGS PATIENTLY WAITING FOR OUR WITS TO GROW SHARPER.

—EDEN PHILLPOTTS

Tadpole Galaxy
Taken in April 2002 by the Hubble's Advanced Camera for Surveys, this image shows the aftermath of a galactic collision. Hidden in the upper left-hand corner of the Tadpole Galaxy is a small blue intruder, which has crossed paths with the larger galaxy causing a massive offshoot of a tail more than 280,000 light-years long. The intruder galaxy is slowly moving away from the Tadpole, leaving a distorted figure in its wake. In the background of the image are points of light that look like stars, but are in reality approximately 6,000 galaxies.

Image: NASA, H. Ford (JHU), G. Illingworth (UCSC/LO), M. Clampin (STScI), G. Hartig (STScI), the ACS Science Team, and ESA

magnificence of all we are setting eyes upon. It reminds us that He alone is God, and He alone is deserving of the glory.

And then to grandeur, we add His grace. Beneath the stars, God's mercy and majesty sing over us together in beautiful harmony, and our souls begin to dance to their music.

Before long we find ourselves echoing the same prayer we heard the writer of Psalm 8 utter—who on Earth are we that the awesome King of all eternity would spare a thought in our direction? Why would the God of yesterday, today, and forever—the One who was, is, and is to come—choose to bestow His loving attention upon the likes of us? The God of unspeakable glory is speaking to us in unmistakable words of love and grace.

Throughout the ages people have been stopping out under the stars. Rich or poor, strong or weak, educated or not, everyone can afford at some point to *stop* and *consider.* In Psalm 19 we hear the starry host making their daily speeches, and night after night projecting brilliant, life-changing knowledge. And then comes a hugely important statement, so relevant to us in this day and age:

> *There is no speech or language where their voice is not heard. (19:3)*

In other words, this star stuff can speak to every age and every culture, at any time in history. No interpreter needed. The heavens have the power to voice the glory of God in all generations. We spend so much time trying to speak relevantly in the various voices of culture—and this is, for sure, a worthwhile pursuit. Yet standing before us, if we'll just stop and consider, is one ready-made, divinely ordained way to point people toward the all-worthy, all-glorious Creator and Sustainer of the universe.

The wonders of the starry host are not merely a masterpiece. They are a message. They are the exquisite proclamations of an unfathomable God. As we lift our eyes, these wonders light up our hearts and pour fuel on the fire of our praise. Every worshipper, indeed, every soul, needs time to simply stop and consider. In the no-nonsense, passionate words of Albert Einstein: "He … who can no longer pause to wonder and stand rapt in awe, is as good as dead."[1]

MR

NOTES:
1. Albert Einstein, quoted in Philip Yancey, *A Skeptic's Guide to Faith* (Grand Rapids, MI: Zondervan, 2009), 13.

R Coronae Australis
The nearby star-forming region around the star R Coronae Australis.

Image and description: ESO

Stellar Cluster NGC 2467
Area surrounding a very active stellar nursery, where new stars are born continuously from large clouds of dust and gas. The bright star at the center of the largest pink region on the bottom of the image is HD 64315, a massive young star that is helping to shape the structure of the whole nebular region.

Image and description: ESO

SYMPHONY

IN REASON'S EAR, THEY ALL REJOICE,
AND UTTER FORTH A GLORIOUS VOICE,
FOREVER SINGING AS THEY SHINE:
"THE HAND THAT MADE US IS DIVINE!"

—JOSEPH ADDISON

WE ALL KNOW THAT STARS SHINE, BUT AS IT TURNS OUT, THEY ALSO SING. EVERY NIGHT (AND ALL DURING THE DAY) the stars are screaming at the top of their lungs, joining creation as they sing to the One who hung them in their places.

When theologian and molecular biophysicist Alister McGrath writes, "It is part of the purpose of the creator that we should hear the music of the cosmos, and, through loving its harmonies, come to love their composer,"[1] he is not writing in poetic terms. If you listen, you can actually hear the stars.

We know stars sing because in our quest to search for extra-terrestrial life (intelligence), we have spent a great deal of time listening to the skies. In the late twentieth century, through a project known as SETI (Search for Extraterrestrial Intelligence), scientists introduced the idea of scanning the sky and listening for nonrandom patterns of electromagnetic emissions, such as radio or television waves, in order to detect another possible civilization somewhere else in the universe. To date, we haven't detected any intelligent life speaking back to us (or speaking at all), but we have heard some amazing stuff.

Large radio telescopes aimed at stars have captured some phenomenal results, including the sounds of the first "singing star" introduced to me—the Vela Pulsar.[2] Eight hundred light-years from Earth, the Vela Pulsar is a highly magnetized neutron star. Exploding into a supernova at death, the Vela collapsed back on itself as a magnetic entity with a force that causes it to rotate ten times per second on its axis.[3]

As it rotates, a radio frequency is emitted (note the blast to the top right of the image). While the whirling Vela is striking to look at, it's incredible to hear as it makes its rhythmic, staccato beat nonstop—a sound we can hear after it travels 800 x 5,800,000,000,000 miles.

But as the Vela taps out a steady beat, other millisecond pulsars hum with the sounds of violins playing in various octaves. 47 Tucanae (47 Tuc), some 16,700 light-years away, is a globular cluster containing a dense concentration of superbright stars. Among them are 23 millisecond pulsars, 16 of which we have recorded.[4] Imagine 16 stringed instruments tuning and playing sustained notes on a massive scale. Who knew that God has His own string section!

The fact that we have recorded sixteen (and identified twenty-three) millisecond pulsars in 47 Tucanae doesn't mean there aren't more. There could be hundreds or millions of other humming wonders in this one globular cluster alone, all singing out His praise.

The psalmist invoked such sounds when he wrote, "Praise him, sun and moon, praise him, all you shining stars" (148:3). And the prophet Nehemiah echoed, "You [God] give life to everything, and the multitudes of heaven worship you" (9:6).

Vela Pulsar
At the center of this image is the Vela Pulsar, a neutron star seen after a supernova explosion. The crossbow shape is caused by hot gases that surround the star, with a jet emerging from one of the star's rotational poles in the upper right-hand corner of the picture.

Image: NASA/CXC/PSU/G. Pavlov et al.

*STARS AND ANGELS SING
AROUND THEE, CENTER
OF UNBROKEN PRAISE.*

—HENRY VAN DYKE

Scientists say that every second, a star somewhere in the universe explodes into a supernova.[5] I wonder what that sounds like? Second after second, day after day, a giant ball of gaseous matter bursts into song—not that each one wasn't singing before it exploded—transmitting its electromagnetic melodies across the heavens. And that doesn't mean that it won't sing again if its end is of the pulsar variety, drumming along with steady praise. It's just that for a moment, each star explodes with such force as to cause the firmament to shudder—fireworks applauding the One who "breathes stars" from nothing into glorious spender.

And praise Him they should. For the natural role of every created thing is to speak up on behalf of its Maker. "In the beginning God created the heavens and the earth" (Gen. 1:1). That's how the Holy Book begins. Yet later, speaking about Christ, it proclaims, "All things were created by him and for him" (Col. 1:16). So given that the stars have their origin in God, they, too, sing their songs for Him. Nightly they tell of His artistry and might in a myriad of ways.

But it's not just a cosmic thing; the whole Earth is in the mix. Psalm 148 continues:

> *Praise the Lord from the earth, you great sea*
> *creatures and all ocean depths, lightning and hail,*
> *snow and clouds, stormy winds that do his bidding,*
> *you mountains and all hills, fruit trees and all cedars,*
> *wild animals and all cattle, small creatures and flying*
> *birds, kings of the earth and all nations, you princes*
> *and all rulers on earth, young men and maidens, old*
> *men and children. Let them praise the name of the*

LORD, *for his name alone is exalted; his splendor is*
above the earth and the heavens. (vv. 7–13)

The psalm writer leaves no stone unturned in describing a great
symphony of epic proportions, one composed of colossal pulsars and
mammoth whales; crashing waves and laughing children; tiny birds
who flap and flutter and thunder's rattling, quaking roll; kings and
commoners, and everything that comes from the hand of God.

As the hymnist Henry Van Dyke wrote, "All Thy works with joy
surround Thee, earth and heaven reflect Thy rays, / Stars and angels
sing around Thee, center of unbroken praise."[6] Seated high above
the heavens, God is central in a universe that performs His magnum
opus.

And somewhere in the midst of it all is you, special among all
of creation, made in the very image of God. Stamped with divinity,
and created in the likeness of God, you, too, were made by and for
Jesus. Thus, you have a voice in the chorus. A voice like no other
because, unlike the stars, you have the capacity to know and love the
Creator—and the choice to value Him above everything else He has
made.

And, unlike the humming pulsars that fill the expanse of space
with their songs, you have been sought after and redeemed. Christ
has come for you, dying and rising to life just to put life and breath
in your lungs again. And He did it not so that you can "punch your
ticket to heaven when you die" but so that you can have something
to sing about that will outshine the heavens.

As crazy as it seems, your voice is not incidental in a universe as
vast as the one we find ourselves in. You are a unique human being,

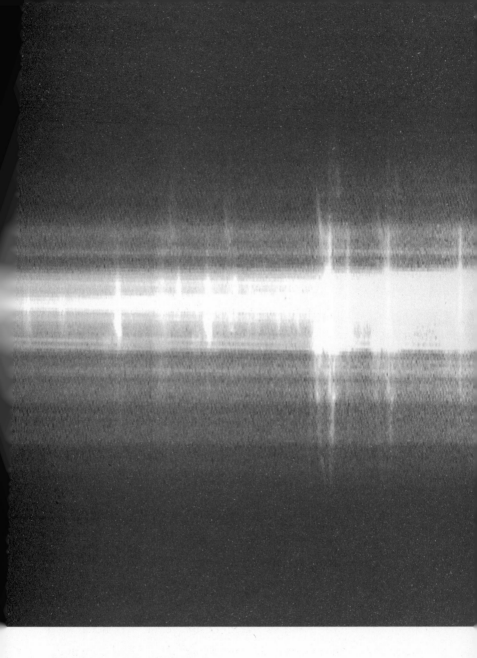

STIS Spectrum of the Variable Star Eta Carina
The Space Telescope Imaging Spectrograph (STIS) is a versatile "combi-instrument" that spreads
out the light gathered by a telescope so that it can be analyzed to determine such properties of
celestial objects as chemical composition and abundances, temperature, radial velocity, rotational
velocity, and magnetic fields.

Image and description: NASA, ESA, and the Hubble SM4 ERO Team

fearfully and wonderful made by the God of all creation. Your praise makes Him smile. First, because He loves you, and second, because He knows that when you're singing His song you've touched and tasted the greatest thing in all the world.

LG

NOTES:

1. Alister McGrath, *Glimpsing the Face of God: The Search for Meaning in the Universe* (Oxford, UK: Lion, 2002), 48.

2. To hear the sounds of the pulsars mentioned in this chapter, visit www.jb.man. ac.uk/~pulsar/Education/Sounds.

3. Robert Nemiroff and Jerry Bonnell, "Astronomy Picture of the Day," *NASA*, June 9, 2000, apod.nasa.gov/apod/ap000609.html.

4. D. R. Lorimer et al., "Millisecond Radio Pulsars in 47 Tucanae," *National Astronomy and Ionosphere Center*, August 2006, www.naic.edu/~pfreire//47Tuc.

5. NASA, ESA, A.V. Filippenko (University of California, Berkeley), P. Challis (Harvard-Smithsonian Center for Astrophysics), et al., "A Bright Supernova in the Nearby Galaxy NGC 2403," *HubbleSite NewsCenter*, September 2, 2004, hubblesite.org/newscenter/archive/releases/2004/23.

6. Henry Van Dyke, "Joyful, Joyful, We Adore Thee" (1907), *Cyber Hymnal*, www.cyberhymnal.org/htm/j/o/joyful.htm.

CH.7 // MATT REDMAN
ASTRONOMICAL GRACE

SO THERE WE WERE—THE CAB DRIVER AND I—SITTING IN BUSY TRAFFIC ON OUR WAY TO THE AIRPORT. BEFORE long, the conversation turned to the universe. Excited at the chance to air some of my most recent star facts, I launched into my spiel:

"Did you know they reckon the Sun is around twenty-seven million degrees Fahrenheit in its unfathomably hot core? And burning up around four million tons of its own mass every second. And it's so huge that even at that rate it would last another five or six billion years."

"Yes, but ..." He tried desperately to get a word in. But I was on a roll:

"Yet they say in many ways the Sun is just a very average star. There are billions of others out there, many of them bigger and brighter than our Sun. In fact—"

"Stop! Stop! You're freaking me out ..." the cab driver interrupted. I was surprised by his outburst. True, I'd bored a few people with my universe trivia before, but this response was unexpected. Intrigued, I listened:

"To be honest," he went on to explain, "this stuff scares me. I try not to think about these things. I'm fascinated by stars and all that—but the sheer scale of things totally unnerves me. It's just too big. It makes me feel so afraid ..."

And that right there is where we differed. For, as a worshipper of Jesus, I find the sheer scale of things inspiring, not terrifying. Yes, it puts the fear and awe of God into me to see these grand designs out there—these measures of creation far beyond our comprehension. And true, it makes me feel miniscule as I stand looking up at the sheer scope of it all. But the more I encounter grandeur, the more I'm drawn into wonder. In the light of these incredible, shining stars, the beauty of the gospel shines ever more brightly in my soul. How could it be that the One who spoke these epic galaxies into being lavishes His love on the likes of you and me? The all-powerful hands of the Maker became the nail-pierced hands of the Savior. He who is everything made Himself nothing. The One who commands the Sun, Moon, and stars in their courses above took on the nature of a servant. The God of creation, who holds all things together, humbled Himself and became obedient to death on a cross. Of all the mysteries of the universe, these are the greatest.

Looking up to the heights of the cosmos increases our sense of the glory of God—and at the same time helps us to realize just how extravagant His divine love is. It is "astronomical grace": the vast, sky-high, off-the-chart wonders of the heart of God.

Even when we see humans expressing grace, it has the power to move us. Think, for example, of the life of the late Princess Diana

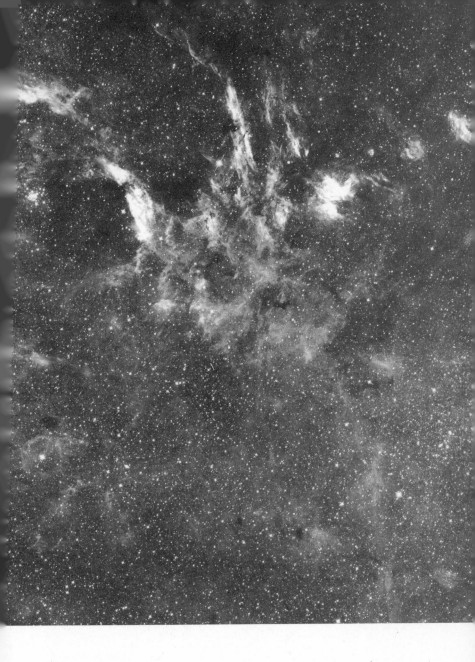

Milky Way's Galactic Core
This sweeping panorama is the sharpest infrared picture ever made of the Milky Way's galactic core, where massive stars are forming.

Hubble image and description: NASA, ESA, and Q. D. Wang
(University of Massachusetts, Amherst), and STScI
Spitzer image: NASA Jet Propulsion Laboratory, and S. Stolovy (Spitzer Science Center/Caltech)

*LOOKING UP TO THE HEIGHTS
OF THE COSMOS INCREASES
OUR SENSE OF THE GLORY
OF GOD—AND AT THE SAME
TIME HELPS US REALIZE
JUST HOW EXTRAVAGANT
HIS DIVINE LOVE IS.*

of Wales. Many a time we saw a newsreel of her reaching out to the wounded, the very poor, or the broken. And it was a powerful picture—a royal princess identifying and getting involved with the lives of those who might never expect to be paid a visit by a person of such power and profile. A tiny picture of human grace. But take it up to the God level, and we encounter grace of epic proportions. How could it be that the Maker of all the universe—these gigantic galaxies stretched out across the heavens—reached out to us, paid us a visit, and identified so powerfully with us at the cross? How could it be that One so mighty made such a merciful bid to become so involved with our lives? The world was so intrigued by the universe that it sent a space shuttle. God so loved the world that He beat us to it and launched His own mission, sending His only Son. The miracle of the Christian gospel is that the One who was quite simply beyond our grasp drew near to us. He who was out of reach reached down to us. At the cross of Jesus Christ, we encounter the one true God on a mission to seek and save the lost. He might simply have impressed us with the soul-inspiring works of His hands, and awed us into sub-mission. Yet our God chose to go much, much further—not simply *wowing* us with greatness, but *wooing* us with grace.

The beautiful truth is this: He who calls out the stars, and names them one by one, knows each of us by name also. It is grace of astro-nomic proportions.

MR

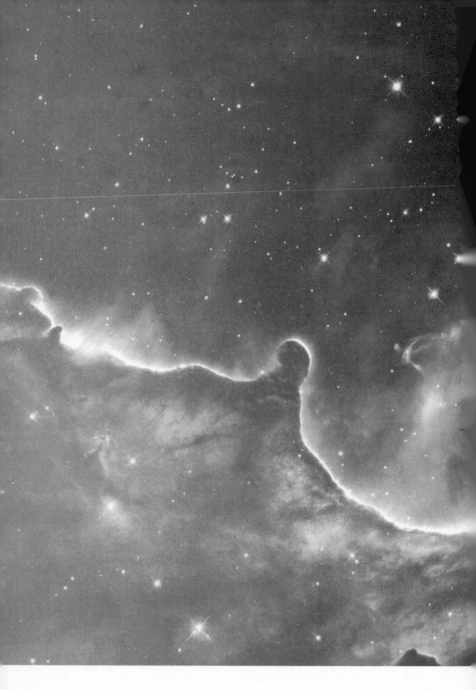

NGC 3324

Image: NASA, ESA, and the Hubble Heritage Team (STScI/AURA)
Acknowledgment: N. Smith (University of California, Berkeley)

NGC 2207

In this image, two huge galaxies are seen interlocked in a battle of gravity. The larger NGC 2207 (left) has distorted the shape of IC 2163 (right), which is flinging debris off to the right side of the image. Eventually, IC 2163 will be forced to give up the fight, and the two galaxies will merge together into one.

Image and description: NASA and the Hubble Heritage Team (STScI)

CH 8 // LOUIE GIGLIO
FAR OUT

BUT IN THESE LAST DAYS [GOD] HAS SPOKEN TO US BY HIS SON, WHOM HE APPOINTED HEIR OF ALL THINGS, AND THROUGH WHOM HE MADE THE UNIVERSE.

—HEBREWS 1:2

THE UNIVERSE IS VAST. IT'S SO BIG, IN FACT, SCIENTISTS AND ASTRONOMERS AREN'T EXACTLY SURE JUST HOW BIG it is. But we know one thing for sure: Measurements like the yard or the mile (or the meter and kilometer) are of no value when trying to comprehend the actual breadth of space. To span the heavens we need a bigger ruler.

For such a task scientists use the astronomical unit (AU), which is roughly the mean distance between the Sun and Earth, or nearly ninety-three million miles. However, the most common measurement used with regard to distances in space is the larger light-year, which is how far light travels in one year.

Light, as you know, is *fast,* screaming along at 186,282 miles per second (299,792 kilometers per second). It's so fast that a beam of light can circle Earth seven times in one second. Traveling nonstop for 365 days, light covers a distance of about 5.8 trillion miles. If you need zeros, a light-year is approximately equal to 5,800,000,000,000 miles. So when we hear that a certain celestial feature or body is

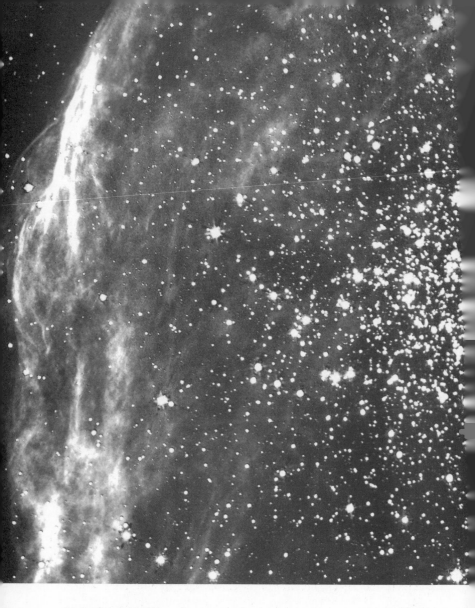

Double Cluster NGC 1850
The double cluster NGC 1850, found in one of our neighboring galaxies, the Large Magellanic Cloud, is a young, "globular-like" star cluster—a type of object unknown in our own Milky Way Galaxy. NGC 1850 is surrounded by a filigree pattern of diffuse gas, which scientists believe was created by the explosion of massive stars.

Image and description: NASA, ESA, Martino Romaniello (European Southern Observatory, Germany), and STScI

Acknowledgments: The image processing for this image was done by Martino Romaniello, Richard Hook, Bob Fosbury, and the Hubble European Space Agency Information Center.

8,000 LY (light-years) from Earth, we are talking about a distance of 8,000 x 5,800,000,000,000 miles.

Just to put the universe in perspective here, the distance between you and the Sun is 1 AU, or 93 million miles. But the distance from the Sun to the next closest star, Proxima Centauri, is 4.3 light-years, or 270,000 times the distance between Earth and the Sun.[1] The stellar disk of the Milky Way Galaxy, our astronomical neighborhood, is somewhere in the range of 100,000–120,000 light-years across and 1,000 light-years thick.[2]

But the Milky Way is not the whole of space. In fact, to a cosmologist, a galaxy like the Milky Way, which contains hundreds of billions of stars, is the *smallest* thing in the universe worth taking note of.[3] That may be hard for some to swallow, but space is enormous, and we're simply orbiting just one of hundreds of billions of stars in the relatively insignificant Milky Way Galaxy, which is only one of hundreds of billions of other galaxies in a universe that's too big to fully map.

But if you want to do some serious measuring, you need a ruler even bigger than a light-year—a ruler bigger than 5.8 trillion miles. And for that we turn to the parsec (pc), a distance of 3.26 light-years, or about 19 trillion miles. If necessary, astronomers can use the even larger measurement, the megaparsec (Mpc), which is equal to a distance of one million parsecs (or approximately 3,262,000 light-years). Astronomers typically measure the distances between neighboring galaxies and galaxy clusters in megaparsecs. That's a huge unit of measurement, but if you were to ever need a larger ruler still, the gigaparsec (about 3.262 billion light-years, or roughly one-fourteenth of the distance to the horizon of the observable universe) would be standing by to help.

Gigaparsecs (Gpc) are used to measure large-scale structures such as the size of, and distance to, the Sloan Great Wall, a filament of galaxies located about a billion light-years away from Earth. The Wall itself is some 1.37 billion light-years in length, which makes it three times as large as the previous record holder, the CfA2 Great Wall.

Yet, even with a ruler as great as the gigaparsec, we still can't quite take it all in. Not that we aren't trying. Recently, a team at the Harvard-Smithsonian Center for Astrophysics created a 3-D image of the cosmos "out to a distance of 380 million light-years away.... The map, known as the '2MASS Redshift Survey' (2MRS), depicts 95 percent of the sky and is said to be the most complete local map of the universe ever created."[4] No doubt, it's a fantastic achievement. Yet, we are still left with a map of the skies that gets us only a mere 380 million light-years into space.

Just to recap some of these staggering measurements:

> The distance from Los Angeles to New York—
   2,462 miles

> The distance from Earth to the Moon—240,000
   miles

> The distance from Earth to the Sun—93 million
   miles

> 1 light-year—5.8 trillion miles

> The distance from the Sun to the nearest star—
4.3 light-years

> Width of the Milky Way Galaxy—
100,000–120,000 light-years

> Distance from the Milky Way to the nearest
galaxy—2.5 million light-years

> Distance from the Milky Way to the CfA2 Great
Wall—200 million light-years

> Distance from the Milky Way to the Sloan Great
Wall—1 billion light-years

So how much farther can we go? At present, with our very best instruments, we have been able to detect objects in space that are on the order of more than 13 billion light-years from Earth. Recently, a short but astonishingly bright explosion was captured in the night sky. It is believed that the flash occurred "when a star died in a supernova explosion and released a powerful jet of high-energy gamma-ray radiation. The blast shined for a mere 10 seconds but packed as much light into the explosion as several thousand galaxies (more than a million million times the brightness of the sun)." While scientists haven't determined precisely where this explosion happened, estimates place it at 13.14 billion light-years away, "making it potentially the farthest object yet detected in space."[5]

Observed by NASA's *Swift* satellite in April 2009, this massive explosion was named GRB 090429B. Some believe the star that caused the explosion lives near the edge of the universe as we know it. "The galaxy hosting the progenitor star of GRB 090429B was truly one of the first galaxies in the universe," said co-researcher Derek Fox, an astronomer at Penn State University. "Beyond the possible cosmic distance record, GRB 090429B illustrates how gamma-ray bursts can be used to reveal the locations of massive stars in the early universe and to track the processes of early galaxy and star formation that eventually led to the galaxy-rich cosmos we see around us today."[6]

But hold on to your telescopes, there is actually something out there that is beyond GRB 090429B. Something really, really far out—so far out that it boggles the mind more than anything we have seen.

What's really far out?

Jesus Christ, hanging on a cross for the sins of the world.

Nothing is more far out than to see the One who made it all and the One who spoke the world into being offering His own life as sacrifice for all the wrongs of every person who ever lived.

Jesus isn't simply the Son of God. He is God. And through Him the universe was created.

Throughout Scripture, God describes His creative work:

> I am the LORD, who has made all things, who alone
> stretched out the heavens, who spread out the earth by
> myself. (Isa. 44:24)

HANDS THAT FLUNG STARS INTO SPACE, TO CRUEL NAILS SURRENDERED.

—*GRAHAM KENDRICK*

> *My own hands stretched out the heavens; I marshaled*
> *their starry hosts. (Isa. 45:12)*

> *By faith we understand that the universe was formed*
> *at God's command, so that what is seen was not made*
> *out of what was visible. (Heb. 11:3)*

Yet, more specifically, Scripture reveals that Jesus is the creative force behind it all.

> *Through him all things were made; without him*
> *nothing was made that has been made. (John 1:3)*

> *For by him all things were created: things in heaven*
> *and on earth, visible and invisible … all things were*
> *created by him and for him. (Col. 1:16)*

> *But in these last days he [God] has spoken to us by*
> *his Son, whom he appointed heir of all things, and*
> *through whom he made the universe. (Heb. 1:2)*

So while it's stunning that we can glimpse a solar burst some thirteen billion light-years away, it's far more incredible that the One who fashioned that star and our own galaxy, and everything seen and unseen throughout the universe, would step onto planet Earth on a rescue mission that defies the odds.

When our foolish rebellion separated us from the God who formed us to both know and love Him forever, Jesus, who said,

"Let there be light," spoke up for you and me. And in the end, in human skin, the sinless and perfect Son of God exchanged His life for every twisted thing that we have done. In that single act, the star breather became the sin bearer. The universe maker became humanity's Savior. It truly is, as Matt has stated so well, astronomical grace.

After all, you really can't use the AU, or the light-year, or the parsec to measure God's love for us. For that, all you need is a cross that's large enough to hold the Son of God.

LG

NOTES:

1. NASA High Energy Astrophysics Science Archive Research Center, "The Nearest Star," heasarc.nasa.gov/docs/cosmic/nearest_star_info.html.
2. Jerry Coffey, "How Big Is the Milky Way," *Universe Today,* October 14, 2010, www.universetoday.com/75691/how-big-is-the-milky-way.
3. John Gribbin, *Hyperspace: Our Final Frontier* (DK, 2001), 21.
4. Alex Eichler, "The Most Complete Map of the Universe," *The Atlantic Wire,* May 26, 2011, www.theatlanticwire.com/technology/2011/05/most-complete-map-universe/38187.
5. Clara Moskowitz, "Huge Space Explosion Is Farthest Thing Ever Seen," *Space.com,* May 25, 2011, www.space.com/11785-space-explosion-farthest-object-grb-090429b-aas218.html.
6. Derek Fox, quoted in "New Candidate for Most Distant Object in the Universe," *EarthSky,* May 28, 2011, earthsky.org/space/new-candidate-for-most-distant-object-in-the-universe.

A 340-Million-Pixel Starscape of the Milky Way
The second of three images of ESO's GigaGalaxy Zoom project is a new and wonderful 340-million-pixel vista of the central parts of our galactic home. The dusty lane of our Milky Way runs obliquely through the image, dotted with remarkable bright, reddish nebulae, such as the Lagoon and the Trifid Nebulae, as well as NGC 6357 and NGC 6334. This dark lane also hosts the very center of our galaxy, where a supermassive black hole is lurking.

Image and description: ESO/S. Guisard

Orion Nebula

NASA's Spitzer and Hubble Space telescopes teamed up to expose the chaos that baby stars are creating 1,500 light-years away in a cosmic cloud called the Orion Nebula. This striking composite indicates that four monstrously massive stars, collectively called the "Trapezium," at the center of the cloud may be the main culprits in the Orion constellation.

Also known as M42, or NGC 1976, Orion is one of the brightest nebulae, containing more than 1,000 young stars.

CH 9 // LOUIE GIGLIO
GLORIOUS DEATH

*WHEN THEY DISCOVER THE CENTER OF THE
UNIVERSE,
A LOT OF PEOPLE WILL BE DISAPPOINTED
TO DISCOVER THEY ARE NOT IT.*

—BERNARD BAILEY

AT THE END OF THE DAY, ALL STARS DIE. COMPOSED MOSTLY OF HYDROGEN GAS, STARS GENERATE ENERGY BY combining hydrogen atoms into helium atoms through a process called fusion. The star slowly releases the resulting radiation from its core, providing the energy needed to sustain it (which allows the star to burn, or shine) for billions of years.

Over time, a star exhausts its fuel as heavier elements form and the star contracts, becoming a white dwarf on the order of most of the stars we see shining in the night sky. Eventually, the white dwarf will cool down and turn into a black dwarf, which has no light or heat. However, this process takes so long, it's believed that no star in our universe has reached this stage.[1]

Red giant stars experience a more creative demise, shedding their outer layers of dust and gas in a round shape that resembles a planet when glimpsed in earthbound telescopes. However, when seen through Hubble's superior lenses, these dust and gas clouds, called planetary nebulae, and other similar supernova remnants

appear in random, whimsical shapes composed of vibrant and varied colors.

Who knew that death could be such a glorious thing, producing some of the most mesmerizing spectacles in the heavens? And we're not talking small-scale, Earth-sized glory here; some of these nebula clouds defy description. Some of the "death-bed" phenomena of these stars are so massive and powerful that they stretch the limits of our ability to comprehend.

For example, the Eagle Pillar Cloud is a cloud-like tower of gas stretching 9.5 light-years (about 57 trillion miles) above the Eagle Nebula. One of NASA's most famous photos of the Eagle Pillar Cloud is called "The Pillars of Creation." This "pillar cloud" alone is just a tiny fraction of the entire nebula, though it's many times the size of our entire solar system.[2]

Then there's Supernova 1987A, one of the brightest supernovae seen in over four hundred years of astronomy and research. Appearing in this photo as a ring of glowing pearls, for a few months this supernova burned over one hundred million times brighter than our own Sun.[3] Not bad for a dying star. The Advanced Camera for Surveys on the Hubble Space Telescope captured this image in November 2003, just as a shock wave released during the explosion collided with a ring of gas while traveling more than a million miles per hour.

Eagle Pillar Cloud
This cloud-like column is a tower of gas rising from the Eagle Nebula. The pillar is made up of hydrogen, oxygen, and dust that is being constantly shaped and formed by the surrounding stars. This cloud is no small phenomenon; the tower is 9.5 light-years (about 57 trillion miles) tall. In the center, the protrusions and bumps that jut out from the main body are roughly the size of our entire solar system.

Image: NASA, ESA, and the Hubble Heritage Team (STScI/AURA)

Consider the "Red Rectangle," another image of a dying star that has baffled astronomers for years. While most nebulae take some rounded or oval shape, this dying star is unique amid its stellar neighbors. Recent close-up images reveal that this stunning wonder was actually formed by two core stars orbiting each other every ten and a half months. Scientists believe that the death of one of the stars caused a vast ring of dust to emerge around both stars, squeezing ejected mass out both sides at an irregular rate, creating the rectangular shape and the squared "rungs" within it.[4]

I could go on sharing images and descriptions of the breathtaking nebulae and supernovae that tax our understanding. But the irony is that if these stars were still in their midlife stages, they wouldn't have made it into the pages of this book or into our imaginations. Their beauty is in their death, a paradox that can also be true in you and me. I'm not referring to our literal deaths, although that moment can certainly be glorious if we have lived lives of faith and trust in Jesus. I'm talking about dying to ourselves while we're still alive. This "death by choice" frees us from our own small and fading stories, allowing our days to count for something much larger and more enduring than we alone could ever be.

It's been said that everybody wants to go to heaven, but nobody wants to die. Many of us seem determined to do whatever it takes to stay alive for as long as possible. And if we're not careful, we'll push ourselves to the center of our own little galaxies. We'll do what we're all prone to do: get whatever stuff we can and hold onto whatever we get for as long as possible.

Yet in the stars, we see beauty in dying. And in their Maker, we see the most glorious death of all. Christ made everything and owns

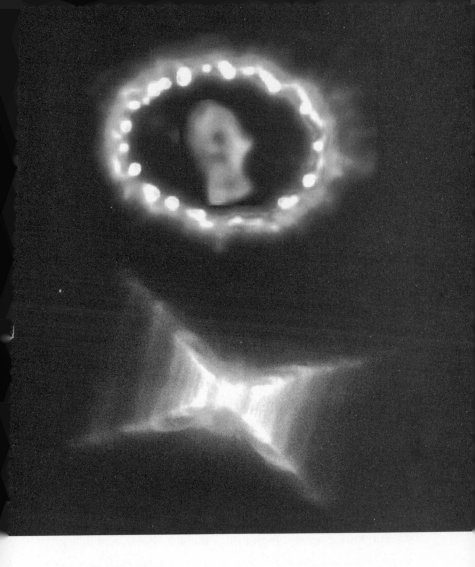

Supernova Shock Wave (Top)

In February 1987, astronomers witnessed the brightest supernova seen in over four hundred years. This burst of light, labeled SN 1987A, was over a hundred million times brighter than the Sun for several months. A shock wave that was released during the explosion collided with a ring of gas at more than a million miles per hour, heating the gas and producing the ring of lit "pearls."

Image: NASA, P. Challis, R. Kirshner (Harvard-Smithsonian Center for Astrophysics), and B. Sugerman (STScI)

Red Rectangle (Bottom)

Located about 2,300 light-years from Earth, the famous "Red Rectangle" is actually formed by two stars at the core that orbit each other every 10½ months. Due to the death of one of these stars, a vast ring of dust has emerged around the stars, squeezing ejected mass out of both sides, creating the rectangular shape.

Image: NASA, ESA, Hans Van Winckel (Catholic University of Leuven, Belgium), and Martin Cohen (University of California, Berkeley)

everything, yet He chose to give Himself away as a peace offering for all humanity. But beyond this, He chose to take our blows, to carry our shame, to bear sin's weight, and suffer in death. And as gruesome as His last hours were, Jesus' death is still the most beautiful thing I've ever seen.

His death brought me life and brought an entire rebel tribe back from the dead. That's why He could say with confidence, "Whoever wants to save [hold onto or hoard] his life will lose it, but whoever loses his life for me [and my kingdom] will find it" (Matt. 16:25).

In other words, those who cling to life with clenched fists, as though it is theirs to do with as they choose, will in the end have nothing but a brief and momentary existence. But those who get over themselves, shed their self-centeredness and self-absorption like the gas and dust shrugged off by a fading star, will find themselves on the doorstep of something more. Losing selfishness for otherness, replacing getting with giving, and uprooting our fame for a passion to spread His name will ensure that our lives endure, both now and for eternity.

But what does that look like? I think it begins with a simple prayer: *Jesus, I want my life, my words, my actions, my thoughts, and all I hold dear to reflect Your glory today. I'm less interested in people seeing me and desire far more that people will see You in me.*

You might ask, "Why would I pray a prayer like that? Am I supposed to be down on myself?"

Quite the opposite. As we have mentioned throughout these pages, you are prized by the God of all creation, more valuable to Him and more deeply loved by Him than you can fully know. But you are just you, finite and frail, unable to exert supernatural power. Unable to come through for every person, in every instance, with every answer.

But, we know the One who has breathed out the stars. Who is faithful and true. The One whose power knows no end. Whose voice brings forth the morning. Why would we want people staring at us, when they could see glimpses of Him?

In the end, dying is simply less of me and more of Jesus. Less trying. Less striving. Less strutting. And more trusting. More surrender. More of His power, doing in and through us what only He can do.

Life is brief, and there's nothing more exhausting than living out our days as if we are the center of the universe, responsible for everything and everybody under the Sun. I think that's why God decided to shroud our nights (and days) in an expansive canopy of wonder, a curtain of shimmering lights reminding us that life is not about you and me but about Someone greater … Someone far brighter than us all.

So don't be afraid to die. Your greatest glory is not a greater you, but you radiating more of His great light.

LG

NOTES:

1. Theo Koupelis, *In Quest of the Stars and Galaxies* (Sudbury, MA: Jones and Bartlett, 2011), 409.
2. NASA, "Eagle Nebula: Closeup," *Space Math,* spacemath.gsfc.nasa.gov/weekly/6Page16.pdf.
3. Nigel Henbest and Heather Couper, *The Guide to the Galaxy* (New York: Cambridge University Press, 1994), 39.
4. Robert Roy Britt, "Rectangular Nebula's True Nature Revealed," *MSNBC,* May 11, 2004, www.msnbc.msn.com/id/4953165/ns/technology_and_science-space/t/rectangular-nebulas-true-nature-revealed.

Debris from Supernova Remnant
Resembling the puffs of smoke and sparks from a summer fireworks display, these delicate filaments are actually sheets of debris from a stellar explosion in a neighboring galaxy. This seemingly gentle structure also harbors a very powerful spinning neutron star that may be the central remnant from the initial blast. In the case of N 49, not only is the neutron star spinning at a rate of once every eight seconds, it also has a super-strong magnetic field a thousand trillion times stronger than Earth's magnetic field.

Image and description: NASA and the Hubble Heritage Team (STScI/AURA)
Acknowledgment: Y.-H. Chu (UIUC), S. Kulkarni (Caltech), and R. Rothschild (UCSD)

Solar Blast
The Sun unleashed an M-2 (medium-sized) solar flare with a spectacular coronal mass ejection (CME) on June 7, 2011. The large cloud of particles mushroomed up and fell back down looking as if it covered an area of almost half the solar surface.

Image and description: Solar Dynamics Observatory

CH 10 // MATT REDMAN
STARING AT THE SUN

WAKING UP ON A TOUR IN DURBAN, SOUTH AFRICA, I PREPARE MYSELF FOR ANOTHER DAY LIVING UNDER THE power of the sun.

Sunglasses … check. Hat … check. Sunblock … check. You can't take any chances when you're about to have an encounter with such a powerful star. Of course, when I say "encounter," I'll still be standing ninety-three million miles away. Yet somehow, that's not quite enough to avoid the force of its extraordinarily powerful rays.

As Thomas Dubay writes, "It would take a jet plane flying from the Sun's surface at 500 miles per hour well over a month … to reach this star's center." At the same time, it's blazing so violently that "to produce the observed energy being emitted from the solar surface, the equivalent of a hundred billion hydrogen bombs must be exploding every second in its unfathomably hot, dense core."

Or, to convey it another way, it would take

the gross national product of the United States for
7 million years ... for your local power company
to run the Sun for a mere second.[1]

Here in South Africa, temperatures might top one hundred degrees Fahrenheit on a hot day. Pretty sweltering (especially if, like me, you are from England). The Sun, on the other hand, will keep scorching away at the unimaginable temperature of twenty-seven million degrees Fahrenheit in its fiercely raging center.

This gigantic ball of gas—70 percent hydrogen—is a fiery furnace, burning up around four million tons of its own mass every single second.[2] Though in some ways an ordinary star, this is no average ball of gas; to us it is life or death. Among its many effects, it keeps us from freezing to death. Its heat and light enable plants to grow, and in turn provide us with food.

No one can escape the influence of the Sun. Even the most powerful people on Earth find themselves living beneath its sway. In April 1984, the late Ronald Reagan, then president of the United States, was on *Air Force One* heading for a meeting with the premier of China. Shortly into the flight, while Reagan was talking with his aides, the lines went dead—and Reagan was informed that all contact had been lost with the world beneath him. As it turned out, the cause had nothing to do with man-made communications.

Push and Pull of Plasma
SDO zoomed in on an interesting display of magnetic forces at work as strands of plasma were tugged back and forth over three days (May 23–25, 2011) above the Sun's surface. Complex magnetic forces were pulling the material along magnetic field lines. We are observing ionized helium at about sixty thousand degrees Celsius in extreme ultraviolet light.

Image and description: Solar Dynamics Observatory

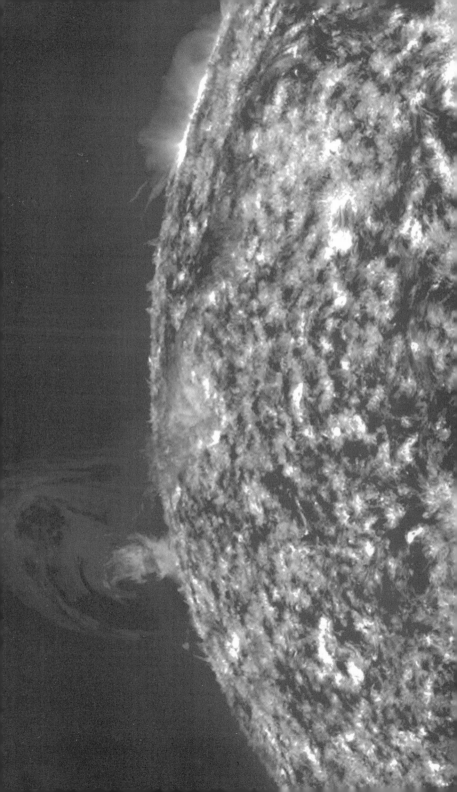

The problem was the Sun in effect "burping," as a series of sunspots exploded out from its surface. Spewing out a trillion kilograms of gas into space, the Sun was messing with Earth's magnetic field and causing widespread communication disruptions throughout Earth that day. And headed for China, even *Air Force One* was not exempt. There on board sat arguably the world's most powerful man—under the authority of a far greater power—our Sun.[3]

In Job, perhaps the oldest book in the Bible, the Sun is used as a picture of the might and radiance of a greater power still—our God. In chapter 37 we read:

> *Now no one can look at the sun, bright as it is in*
> *the skies after the wind has swept them clean. Out of*
> *the north he comes in golden splendor; God comes in*
> *awesome majesty. The Almighty is beyond our reach*
> *and exalted in power. (vv. 21–23)*

These are amazing poetic lines, in which the natural speaks of the supernatural. The writer points us to the glories of the Sun—only that he might lead us on to greater glories—the power, strength, and splendor of the One who called it into being.

The New Testament, as well, uses descriptions of the Sun to point us toward the splendor of God. The writer of Revelation finds that there are simply no words to describe the glory of the One he's encountering. Faced with the astounding light of the risen and ascended King Jesus, he can attempt to describe Him only in relation to the brightest thing he's seen up until that point in his life:

His face was like the sun shining in all its brilliance.
(Rev. 1:16)

In other words, "So, you think the *Sun* is bright? You should see the *Son*."

One day, every tribe and tongue will find themselves staring at the *Son*. On that day, every heart will recognize and respond to King Jesus for who He truly is. On that day too, those who chose Him on Earth will realize that the Sun they saw in the sky every day was merely a temporary necessity. For, as Revelation 21:23 inspires us, our heavenly dwelling will have no need for the Sun—"for the glory of God gives it light, and the Lamb is its lamp." What an astounding thought.

MR

CONSIDER THIS

- "A pinhead heated to the temperature of the center of the Sun would emit enough heat to kill anyone who ventured within a thousand miles of it."[4]

- "The luminosity (intrinsic brightness) of the Sun is 4 x 1019 (40 billion billion) megawatts. Putting this into perspective, the total human consumption of power on Earth is about 2 million megawatts."[5]

Full View of the Sun
This sonogram-type imaging of the solar farside (the side of the Sun not facing Earth) from SOHO/MDIAbstract has been improved to provide a more complete view of the farside. This is important in space weather forecasting as it enables us to see large sunspots and active regions before they are visible directly from Earth.

Image and description: NASA/Goddard Space Flight Center Scientific Visualization Studio

- "The sun's rays may seem weightless to us, but all the photons falling on Earth at every moment weigh as much as a large ocean liner."[6]

- "99.9% of all matter in our solar system is contained within the Sun."[7]

- The temperature of the Sun's surface is 10,832 degrees Fahrenheit. Each inch burns with the brightness of 650,000 candles.[8]

NOTES:

1. Thomas Dubay, *The Evidential Power of Beauty: Science and Theology Meet* (San Francisco: Ignatius, 1999), 133–36.
2. Charles Cardona, *Star Clusters: A Pocket Field Guide* (New York: Springer, 2010), 6.
3. David Whitehouse, *The Sun: A Biography* (Indianapolis: Wiley, 2005), 3–4.
4. James Jeans, quoted in K. C. Cole, *The Universe and the Teacup: The Mathematics of Truth and Beauty* (San Diego: Harcourt, 1997), 20.
5. Charles Robert O'Dell, *The Orion Nebula: Where Stars Are Born* (Cambridge, MA: Harvard University Press, 2003), 59.
6. Dubay, 136.
7. John Scalzi, *The Rough Guide to The Universe* (London: Rough Guides, 2003), 31.
8. John Farndon, *1000 Facts on SPACE.* (New York: Barnes and Noble, 2001).

THAT YOU MAY BE BLAMELESS AND INNOCENT, CHILDREN OF GOD WITHOUT BLEMISH IN THE MIDST OF A CROOKED AND TWISTED GENERATION, AMONG WHOM YOU SHINE AS LIGHTS IN THE WORLD, HOLDING FAST TO THE WORD OF LIFE.

—PHILIPPIANS 2:15–16 (ESV)

THE GLORY OF THE MOON IS THE SUN.

Without the Sun, the Moon would be just another ball of rock and dust floating through space. But to its credit, the Moon is covered with regolith, or lunar dust, which is silvery in color and reflective in nature. This surface material reflects the bright rays of sunlight from our nearest star, causing the Moon to glow gloriously in the night sky.

Sunlight reflected from the Moon's surface takes only 1.3 seconds to reach us here on Earth, over 238,900 miles (384,500 kilometers) away.[1] That's quick, especially when you consider that making the same Earth-Moon journey by car, traveling nonstop around the clock at 80 miles per hour, would take 124 days. Light, traveling 186,000 miles per second, makes the journey quickly, but it is the unique quality of the lunar regolith that makes the reflection stunningly bright.

In fact, when the Moon is full, you can hardly miss it. At least, that's what you'd think …

Earth and the Moon
The Galileo spacecraft returned these images of Earth and the Moon in 1992 on its way to explore the Jupiter system. Separate images of Earth and the Moon were combined to generate this view.
Image: NASA, JPL

Somewhere around midnight, our small twin-engine King Air took flight, climbing into the night sky above Houston, Texas, carrying us home. The plane's owner had been gracious enough to offer us a lift back to Waco after my regular Sunday night speaking engagement at a church in the city. Accompanying Shelley and me were two friends who were going to make the return trip with the pilot back to Houston.

Exhausted from a long day, I was quietly tracking our progress as we flew over the sprawling suburbs when I noticed some kind of crime-scene drama unfolding on the streets below. Though I couldn't tell exactly what was going on, it appeared a car chase was taking place, as I could see a bright circular beam of light from a police helicopter racing across the ground.

I couldn't see the source of the searchlight, or get a bearing on the bandit(s), but I easily followed the light's course as its white circle fled across parking lots and through neighborhood streets. After a few minutes, I closed my eyes and went back to minding my own business.

It wasn't long before a little bump of turbulence opened my eyes. We now flew over open land beyond the city; dark fields passed by below us. As I looked down again, I was surprised to see the searchlight below. What was going on? What were they looking for? Who were they following into the sparse countryside?

Eager to report the spectacle, I interrupted the onboard conversation with the following announcement: "I know it sounds weird," I interjected in my usual understated way, "but there's some kind of police search happening down below us. I've been following this searchlight since we left Houston. I'm not sure what's going on, but I thought you guys would like to know."

After a collective "oh, cool," everyone went right back to whatever it was they were talking about before. All except for the pilot, who, with total disdain for my ignorance, replied, "Well, actually that's not a searchlight below us, buddy. If you'll look up, you'll see there's a full Moon out tonight."

My eyes darted upward, and I saw the brightest, most massive full Moon you can imagine hanging conspicuously overhead.

With a slight dramatic pause, and a lecturer's tone, he continued, "So what's happening here is the moonlight is shining on the plane and reflecting onto the ground. That's why that light you see looks like it's following us. That little circle you see is actually not a searchlight, it's moonlight."

"Oh, yeah, I see it now.… Thanks for the heads-up."

Uggh.

How could I have been so preoccupied with looking down that I missed the enormous full Moon above? Needless to say, I felt like an idiot. The next few minutes were awkwardly silent.

Sensing a mixture of pity and embarrassment from everyone, I just sat there looking up into the sky, when out of nowhere a bolt of inspiration hit me. Armed with newfound confidence, I calmly added:

"Well, I get what you're saying, but actually there's something else going on out there. That's not moonlight reflecting off the plane after all. If you think about it, it's really the light of the Sun, reflecting off the Moon. So technically speaking, it's not the Moon, but the Sun that's shining on the plane and reflecting down to the ground. So that's sunlight, not moonlight, I've been seeing on the ground all this time."

I have to admit, it was a desperate attempt to avoid looking so dumb, but this Sun-Moon-Earth thing was a minirevelation that had huge implications for me. That night, a simple yet paradoxical thought became crystal clear: The Sun shines at night when the Moon is in the right place.

Without the Moon, night is as it's supposed to be: dark and foreboding. But when the Moon is full, night can actually be quite bright.

On these occasions, something called *retroreflection* occurs, meaning the Moon is reflecting light back toward its source: the Sun. When the Moon is full, the Sun is at our backs, allowing earthbound observers to see the full effect of the retroreflective phenomenon.[2] This phenomenon is highlighted by the lunar dust, which reflects light more brightly than many other surface materials would.

When full, the Moon lights the night, inspires romantics, perhaps induces labor, and some say even incites violence. We remark, "Oh, my goodness, did you happen to see the Moon last night.... It was so beautiful." The Moon seems to get all the credit, but it's the Sun that does all the work.

That's what happened recently when what's called a *supermoon* made headlines around the globe. A full Moon at maximum perigee (that moment when the Moon's elliptical orbit brings it closest to Earth), this supermoon appeared 14 percent wider and 30 percent brighter than a normal full Moon as it rose over the evening horizon.[3] Once again, all the buzz was about the Moon. No one seemed to care that the Sun radiated with such ferocious energy that it brilliantly lit the Moon from over ninety-three million miles away!

Moon Image 1 (Top)
Taken by the Apollo 8 astronauts, this image captures parts of the Moon that most people will never physically see. The right half of the Moon, in this image, is part of the lunar farside, the side of the Moon that always faces away from Earth.
Image: NASA Johnson Space Center (NASA-JSC)

Moon Image 2 (Bottom)
The astronauts who had just left the Moon's surface on the Apollo 11 mission took this image of the Moon in full sunlight. At the time, they had already traveled ten thousand nautical miles on their journey home.
Image: NASA Johnson Space Center (NASA-JSC)

Moon Image 3 (Top)
Taken in 1990 by the Galileo Solid State imaging system, this photograph shows the western part of the Moon's nearside. The Copernicus crater, which lies near the center of the encroaching shadow, is sixty miles in diameter.
Image: NASA Jet Propulsion Laboratory (NASA-JPL)

Moon Image 4 (Bottom)
When the Moon and Sun align perfectly with our planet, an image like this can be seen from Earth. This photograph was taken from Merritt Island, Florida, in 2003, and captures the rare moment when the Moon passes directly through the imaginary line that connects Earth and the Sun. The dim light cast on the Moon is actually traveling through Earth's atmosphere.
Image: NASA Kennedy Space Center (NASA-KSC)

The Sun is the true star of the show, while the Moon is simply a bit player. Technically speaking, there is no such thing as moonlight, just sunlight that reaches us in an indirect way. The Sun is a *luminous* object, one capable of emitting light, while the moon is an *illuminated* object, one capable only of reflecting light.

If you think about it, we humans are both luminous and illuminating, spiritually speaking. Without God, we, too, are just balls of dust floating through life. But in Christ, we become both carriers of His divine light and beautiful reflectors of His glory.

> For God, who said, "Let light shine out of darkness,"
> made his light shine in our hearts to give us the light
> of the knowledge of the glory of God in the face of
> Christ. But we have this treasure in jars of clay to
> show that this all-surpassing power is from God and
> not from us. (2 Cor. 4:6–7)

Just as the Sun shines at night when the Moon is in the right place, God shines in the darkness when we are in the right place. When we are in full view of Jesus, His love, grace, goodness, and power directly impact us. In that place, in the brightness of His presence, His light will reflect off us so others can see, no matter how dark the night.

It's amazing to think that, simply by our proximity to Jesus, we can bring hope and life to people and places trapped in discouragement and despair. Though an unsuspecting person may try to give us "moonlight credit," we know that we are not the source, just cracked jars reflecting the miracle of the gospel.

This knowledge means there's no striving on our part, no straining to light the world around us. Only positioning, abiding in the love of Jesus, and letting that love shine in and through us. And there's no time for grabbing glory when light illuminates the darkness.

Every good Moon knows full well that night light comes from the Sun.

LG

NOTES:
1. Evalyn Gates, *Einstein's Telescope: The Hunt for Dark Matter and Dark Energy in the Universe* (New York: Norton, 2009), 28.
2. James S. Trefil, ed., *Encyclopedia of Science and Technology* (New York: Routledge, 2001), 24.
3. Associated Press, "Super Full Moon to Shine on Saturday," *Boston.com*, March 18, 2011, www.boston.com/news/science/articles/2011/03/18/ super_full_moon_to_shine_on_saturday.

Spicules on the Sun
One of the highest resolution images yet of the enigmatic solar flux tubes known as spicules.
Lasting about five minutes, these solar features start out as tall tubes of rapidly rising gas but
eventually fade as the gas peaks and falls back down to the Sun.

Image and description: K. Reardon (Osservatorio Astrofisico di Arcetri, INAF) IBIS, DST, NSO

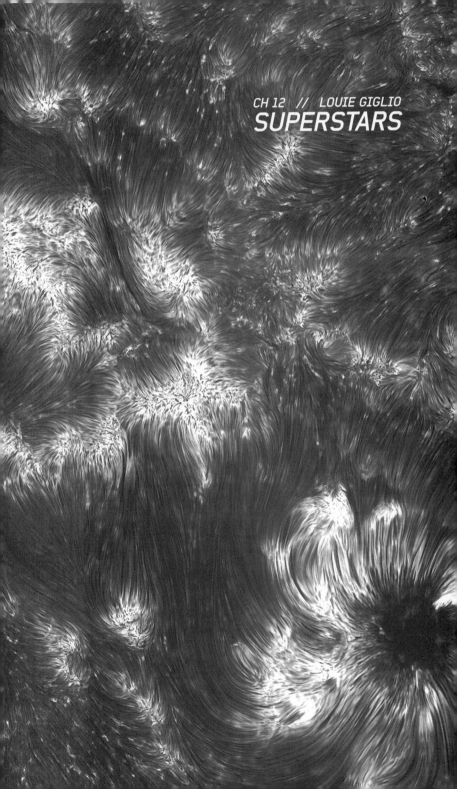

CH 12 // LOUIE GIGLIO
SUPERSTARS

THE SUN IS BIG. AND HOT.

I know that sounds a little simplistic, but let's face it, we mortals have a hard time grappling with the true size of objects that are exponentially larger than us—especially on the scale of the stars.

Everyone knows the Sun is bright, and though it sits a seemingly comfortable ninety-three million miles away, we all respect the intensity of its rays. And yet, we faintly know its terror. We watch it rise and set with glorious splendor, and note its stunning beams as they burst forth from the clouds and glimmer through the trees. But, trust me, the Sun is no gentle giant. It's an orbiting thermonuclear reactor with staggering force and destructive energy.

A paradoxical mystery, "the Sun, with all those planets revolving around it, and depending on it, can still ripen a bunch of grapes as though it had nothing else in the Universe to do."[1] Yet, you shouldn't mistake its life-giving graces for kindness. The star that anchors our very existence is an exploding fireball emitting solar eruptions so forceful any one of them could strip the magnetic information off your credit cards from a distance as far away as the Moon is from Earth. In fact, in 2005, an electromagnetic jolt from a star over fifty thousand light-years away was still strong enough to rock Earth.[2]

Often mistakenly labeled "just an average star," the Sun is actually quite special in many ways. For example, "the Sun is among the 9 percent most massive stars in the Milky Way galaxy." And, when it comes to the stability of light output, the Sun is at the top of the class.[3] Were the Sun, instead of being stable, to have huge swings in output or if it were slightly closer to or farther away from Earth, most likely you wouldn't be reading these words right now.

But what I'd like for us to get our heads around is the actual size of stars, which will help us to consider what that says about the One who makes them. The ancient Scripture tells us that God *breathes out* the stars. "By the word of the Lord were the heavens made, their starry host by the breath of his mouth" (Ps. 33:6). *Wow.* Reading and coming to terms with these words, we instantly know that God isn't our size. He's a beautiful, radiant, limitless, and holy Creator who demands and deserves our awe and devotion.

To put this in perspective, let's take a closer look at just four stars He has made.

We've already talked about our Sun, but how can we grasp its size and scope? Years ago, while working on a message to convey these truths, a friend helped me create a comparison scale for the Sun and even larger stars that allows us to get a better sense of just how gigantic they really are. The comparison scale works like this: If Earth were the size of a golf ball, the Sun would be fifteen feet in diameter. That's a measurement we can actually comprehend, and if you were looking for the ultimate science project, it's on a scale you could reproduce. Taking it a step further, again, if Earth were a golf ball, you could fit close to one million Earths inside the Sun. That would be enough golf balls to fill an entire school bus!

But looking a little deeper into space we find a more massive star called Betelgeuse, which is 427 light-years away. Betelgeuse is so big, in fact, that it's twice the size of Earth's orbit around the Sun.[4] When I first heard that fact as a teenager, it put a serious dent in my prayer life. How do you talk to a God who breathes out stars that huge? To put it in perspective using our comparison scale, if Earth were a golf ball, Betelgeuse would be the size of six Empire State Buildings stacked on top of each other.

What? Imagine going into Manhattan on a busy day, placing your golf ball at the base of the Empire State Building, walking across the block for a better vantage point and seeing five more Empire State Buildings on top of the real one, and then looking all the way back down to your tiny little golf ball on the sidewalk!

If that's not crazy enough, check this out: You could fit 262 trillion Earths inside of Betelgeuse. If Earth were a golf ball, that's enough Earths to fill an indoor football stadium with golf balls—three thousand times!

Hello. God is big. He's much, much bigger than you think.

But let's meet our third star, Mu Cephei. Also known as Hershel's Garnet Star, Mu Cephei is a red supergiant and one of the largest and most luminous stars in our galaxy. Nearing death, Mu Cephei still must be respected. If Earth were the size of a golf ball, Mu Cephei would be as wide as two Golden Gate Bridges stretched end to end. Mu Cephei could hold 2.7 quadrillion Earths!

The last of our four stars, however, dwarfs them all. VY Canis Majoris is appropriately called "the big dog," and while it's 4,900 light-years from Earth, it boasts a diameter of about 1.7 billion miles.[5] To say it another way, the distance around VY Canis Majoris is on the order of 8 to 9 times the 93-million-mile distance from Earth to the Sun.

If Earth were a golf ball, VY Canis Majoris would be the height of Mount Everest.

Hmm. So, if you need some fresh perspective on just how big the God you're praying to is tonight, take an expedition to the top of the planet. Once there, unzip your parka and pull out your golf ball. Standing there on Mount Everest, six miles above sea level, consider for a moment that the golf ball is your home, and just one of the stars that came from the mouth of God is as tall as the mountain beneath your feet.

VY Canis Majoris is so monstrous you could fit seven quadrillion Earths inside it. That's enough Earths, if Earth were a golf ball, to cover the entire state of Texas in golf balls—*two feet deep*. I've lived in Texas, and Texans pride themselves on "big." But try to visualize the whole of Texas covered from end to end in golf balls up to your knees. Now imagine that somewhere among them is one called Earth, and that you're standing on it right now.

Here comes that shrinking feeling again, and we've touched on just four stars among the hundreds of billions *times* hundreds of billion stars that God both created and oversees as He manages the heavens beyond our sight.

So maybe, in light of what we've seen here, a good plan would be to pause more often, turn down the volume of the earthbound

VY CANIS
MAJORIS

MU CEPHEI

BETELGEUSE

SUN

"super-stars" we so quickly gravitate toward, and rest in the shadow of a God who exhales luminous balls of uncontrollable combustion as if they were merely fireflies on a warm summer night.

If the power of the stars is hard to fathom, how much more so is the power of the One who holds them in place beyond our understanding. If His are the arms that are holding you now, rest … and trust. You are in good hands.

LG

NOTES:

1. Attributed to Galileo Galilei, quoted in Michael J. Carlowicz and Ramon E. Lopez, *Storms from the Sun: The Emerging Science of Space Weather* (Washington, DC: Joseph Henry, 2002), 153.
2. Rachel Carr, "Shockwave of X-Ray Starquake Enthralls Scientists," *LiveScience,* February 20, 2009, www.livescience.com/3354-shockwave-ray-starquake-enthralls-scientists.html.
3. Guillermo Gonzalez and Jay Wesley Richards, *The Privileged Planet: How Our Place in the Universe Is Designed for Discovery* (Washington, DC: Regnery, 2004), 137.
4. Arthur I. Miller, *Empire of the Stars: Obsession, Friendship, and Betrayal in the Quest for Black Holes* (New York: Houghton Mifflin, 2005), 55.
5. John Carl Villanueva, "VY Canis Majoris," *Universe Today,* September 8, 2009, www.universetoday.com/39472/vy-canis-majoris.

Starburst Cluster NGC 3603

Like a fireworks display, a young, glittering collection of stars looks like an aerial burst. The cluster is surrounded by clouds of interstellar gas and dust—the raw material for new star formation. The nebula, located twenty thousand light-years away in the constellation Carina, contains a central cluster of huge, hot stars, called NGC 3603.

Image and description: NASA, ESA, R. O'Connell (University of Virginia), F. Paresce (National Institute for Astrophysics, Bologna, Italy), E. Young (Universities Space Research Association/Ames Research Center), the WFC3 Science Oversight Committee, and the Hubble Heritage Team (STScI/AURA)

Spirograph Nebula
About two thousand light-years from Earth, the planetary nebula IC 418 is a beautiful display of history from a dying star. The red giant star in the center of the nebula has ejected its outer layers and is now heating the material it ejected by ultraviolet radiation. This image reveals incredibly intricate texture in the nebula that is still mysterious to astronomers.

Image: NASA and the Hubble Heritage Team (STScI/AURA)
Acknowledgment: Dr. Raghvendra Sahai (JPL) and Dr. Arsen R. Hajian (USNO)

CH 13 // MATT REDMAN

FINELY TUNED

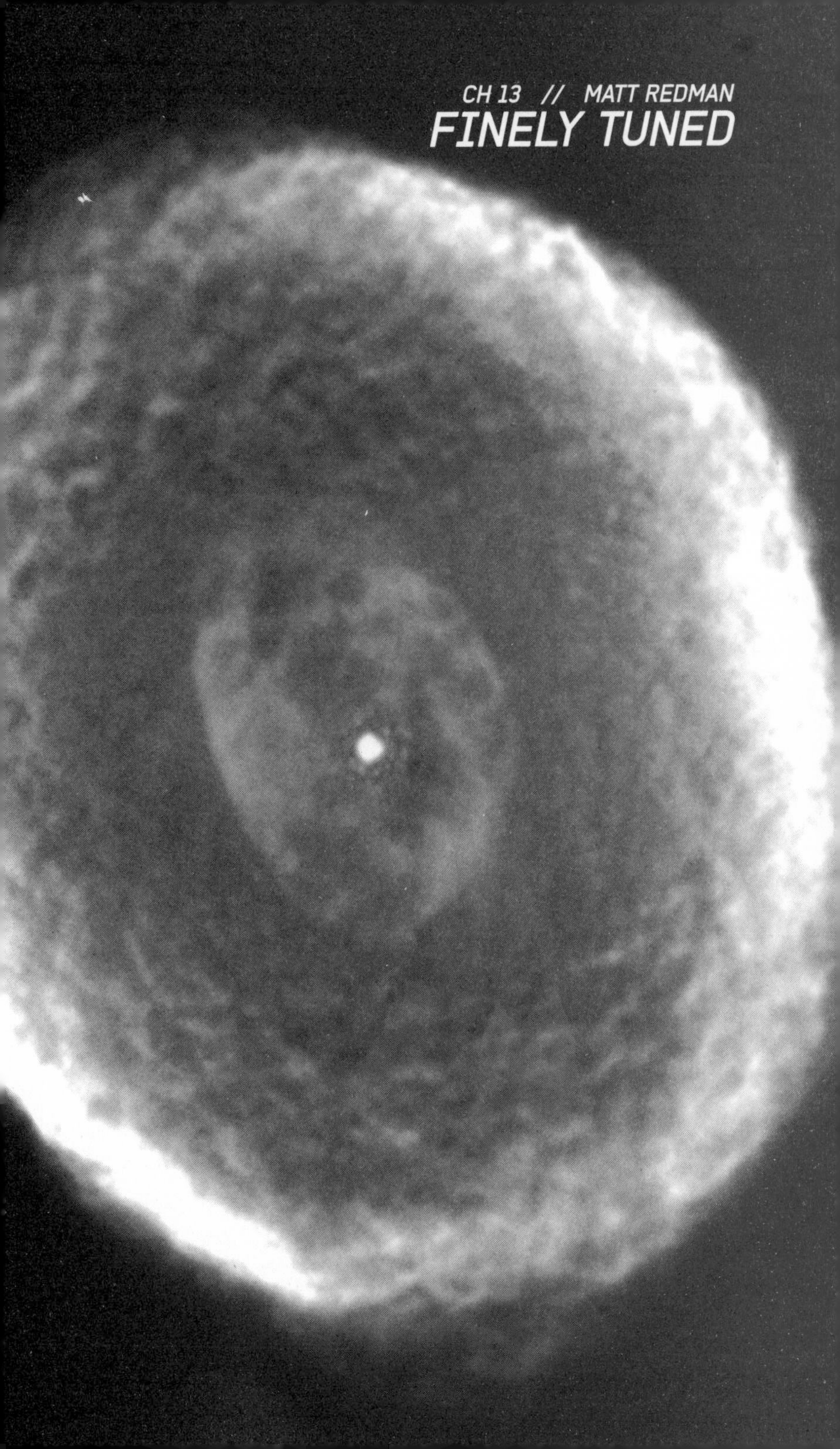

SHAKESPEARE WROTE THAT THE WHOLE WORLD IS A
STAGE. IN ACTUAL FACT, THE WHOLE UNIVERSE IS ONE.
And on display is the dazzling design of a glorious Creator. Yet it's
not simply a shiny outer shell or a thin veneer. Things are just as
impressive when we begin to look behind the scenes. The wonder of
creation is not only that it's so magnificent to behold—but that it's
so masterfully put together. The design of the universe is filled with
harmony, consistency, and elegance. As astrophysicist Paul Davies
writes, "The equations of physics have in them incredible simplicity,
elegance and beauty. That in itself is sufficient to prove to me that
there must be a God who is responsible for these laws and responsible for the universe."[1] Nobel Laureate Arno Penzias echoes the same
thinking:

> Astronomy leads us to a unique event, a universe
> which was created out of nothing and deli-
> cately balanced to provide exactly the conditions

required to support life. In the absence of an
absurdly-improbable accident, the observations
of modern science seem to suggest an underlying,
one might say, supernatural plan.[2]

Scientists these days talk of the "fine-tuning" of nature and the
cosmos. Looking behind the scenes at the laws of physics, they find
a number of constants—which if altered by even tiny degrees would
make the existence of life and order impossible. Even as it is, we look
around and in general see the universe to be a hostile habitat for the
likes of us. But there's one tiny spot we've found that is perfectly
placed for life to thrive. We call it planet Earth.

John O'Keefe, an astronomer at NASA, says: "We are, by
astronomical standards, a pampered, cosseted, cherished group of
creatures.… If the Universe had not been made with the most exact-
ing precision we could never have come into existence. It is my view
that these circumstances indicate the universe was created for man
to live in."[3]

Our planetary home is blessed with the ideal conditions for
life—and it cannot just be blind chance, for the odds are way too
high. There are multiple parameters that scientists identify as essential to the existence of an orderly universe and to the possibility of
life here on Earth. Take, for example, the Sun. If it were too far
away, much of our water would freeze—too near, and it would
boil. Putting this in perspective, Mars (the next planet beyond
us) averages a chilly -81 degrees Fahrenheit, and Venus (our nearest neighbor the other way) hosts temperatures of around 900
degrees.[4] There are other factors too. Were the Sun the wrong kind

THE STATISTICAL PROBABILITY THAT ORGANIC STRUCTURES AND THE MOST PRECISELY HARMONIZED REACTIONS THAT TYPIFY LIVING ORGANISMS WOULD BE GENERATED BY ACCIDENT IS ZERO.

—ILYA PRIGOGINE
NOBEL LAUREATE IN CHEMISTRY

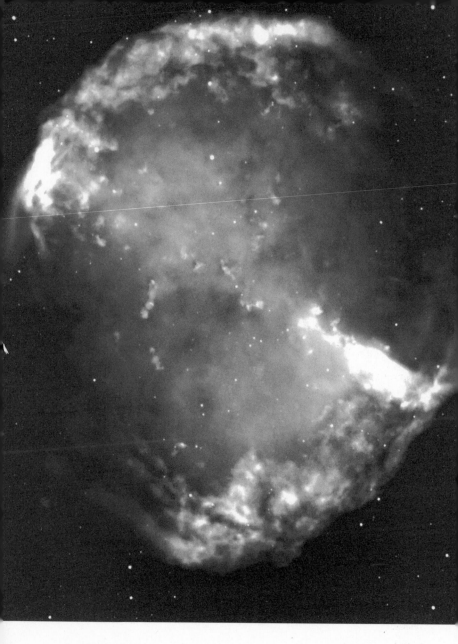

Dumbbell Nebula

The Dumbbell Nebula—also known as M27 or NGC 6853—is a typical planetary nebula and is located in the constellation Vulpecula (The Fox). The distance is rather uncertain, but is believed to be around 1,200 light-years. It was first described by the French astronomer and comet hunter Charles Messier, who found it in 1764 and included it as number 27 in his famous list of extended sky objects.

Image and description: ESO

of radiation source, it wouldn't be stable enough to allow survival. Were it bigger, its luminosity would change too rapidly, creating energy-radiation levels way too high for us. Though it's such a violent figure in our solar system, the Sun's relationship with Earth is just right to sustain life on our planet.

Moving on to Earth itself, it has just the right atmosphere—for if oxygen levels decreased by even a few percent, animals would not be able to breathe. A few percent more, and all plant life would be burned up. Add to this the fact that its size, gravitational pull, magnetic field, and the thickness of its crust are all "just right," and we start to realize just how privileged a planet we live upon.

Yet, when it comes to a finely tuned universe, these examples are merely the tip of the cosmic iceberg. There are many more that further demonstrate the abundance of miraculous design all around us. Scientist Hugh Ross actually identifies more than two dozen parameters in the makeup of the universe that if altered by only narrow amounts would make it impossible for physical life of any kind to exist.[5] To give a picture of this, cosmologists ask us to imagine a universe-creating machine with many dials—each representing one of these parameters. Every dial has a great number of settings—and a tiny change on any one dial would make conditions for life impossible. Astonishingly, every single one seems to be turned to the precise setting for life to exist. Amazing grace, found right in the heart of physics.

When it comes to the structures of the universe, our Almighty God is both Author and Sustainer. He is the One who called it all into being, and the One who keeps everything in place. The Bible tells us of Jesus:

For by him all things were created: things in heaven
and on earth ... and in him all things hold together.
(Col. 1:16–17)

In Jesus Christ *all* things hold together. Not just some things. But *all* things. And encouragingly, that includes our lives. The One who keeps the entire universe together holds our very fragile lives in His ever-capable hands. He who watches over the Sun, Moon, and stars in their courses above also watches over us. Indeed, Scripture tells us that for those who love God "all things work together for good" (Rom. 8:28 esv). Yes, we may look to the design of the universe and discover parameters of physics cooperating to provide for life here on Earth. Yet looking to the details of our own little journeys, we see the same sovereign hand of kindness at work—our Father in heaven working all things together for good in the lives of those who love Him. At times you may feel as though things are spiraling out of control. Life can be messy, and painful, and confusing. But for the heart of anyone holding a deep faith in Christ, there is very good news indeed. For all the shakiness and unpredictability of life, there He stands in the middle, as constant and faithful as He ever was, holding all things together, and holding you in His heart.

In chapter 1 of Revelation, we read of Jesus' holding seven stars in His right hand. Whatever the exact meaning of this, it is a picture of a God who must be wondered at and revered. Indeed, John tells us that when he saw this he "fell at his feet as though dead" (v. 1:17). But the very next words complete the picture and give us a fantastic view of what our God is like. For Jesus takes that same right hand with which He was holding the stars and places it on John, comforting him and saying, "Do not be afraid" (1:17). We see both transcendence and immanence—the God who is utterly and completely set apart is drawing near and working up close in the life of His worshipper. Revere Him, yes. But also rejoice that the God who created the stars is the very same God who draws close and extends a hand of compassion and comfort. Jesus the star-maker is working on your life with His kindness and power, marking your every day with His mercies and His might. Our lives, right here and right now, are being "finely tuned."

MR

NOTES:

1. Paul Davies, *Superforce* (New York: Simon and Schuster, 1984), quoted in Walter L. Bradley, "Nature," in *Mere Creation: Science, Faith, and Intelligent Design,* ed. William A. Dembski (Downers Grove, IL: InterVarsity, 1998), 38.
2. Arno Penzias, quoted in Walter Bradley, "The 'Just So' Universe: The Fine-Tuning of Constants and Conditions in the Cosmos," in *Signs of Intelligence: Understanding Intelligent Design,* eds. William Dembski and James Kushiner (Grand Rapids, MI: Brazos, 2001), 168.
3. John O'Keefe, quoted in Fred Heeren, *Show Me God: What the Message of Space Is Telling Us about God* (Wheeling, IL: Searchlight Publications, 1995), 200.
4. NASA, "The Gas Giants," *FastFacts,* nai.nasa.gov/habitabilitycards.pdf.
5. Hugh Ross, *The Creator and the Cosmos* (Colorado Springs: NavPress, 2001), 154. For additional reading, see www.reasons.org.

CH 14 // MATT REDMAN

BEYOND

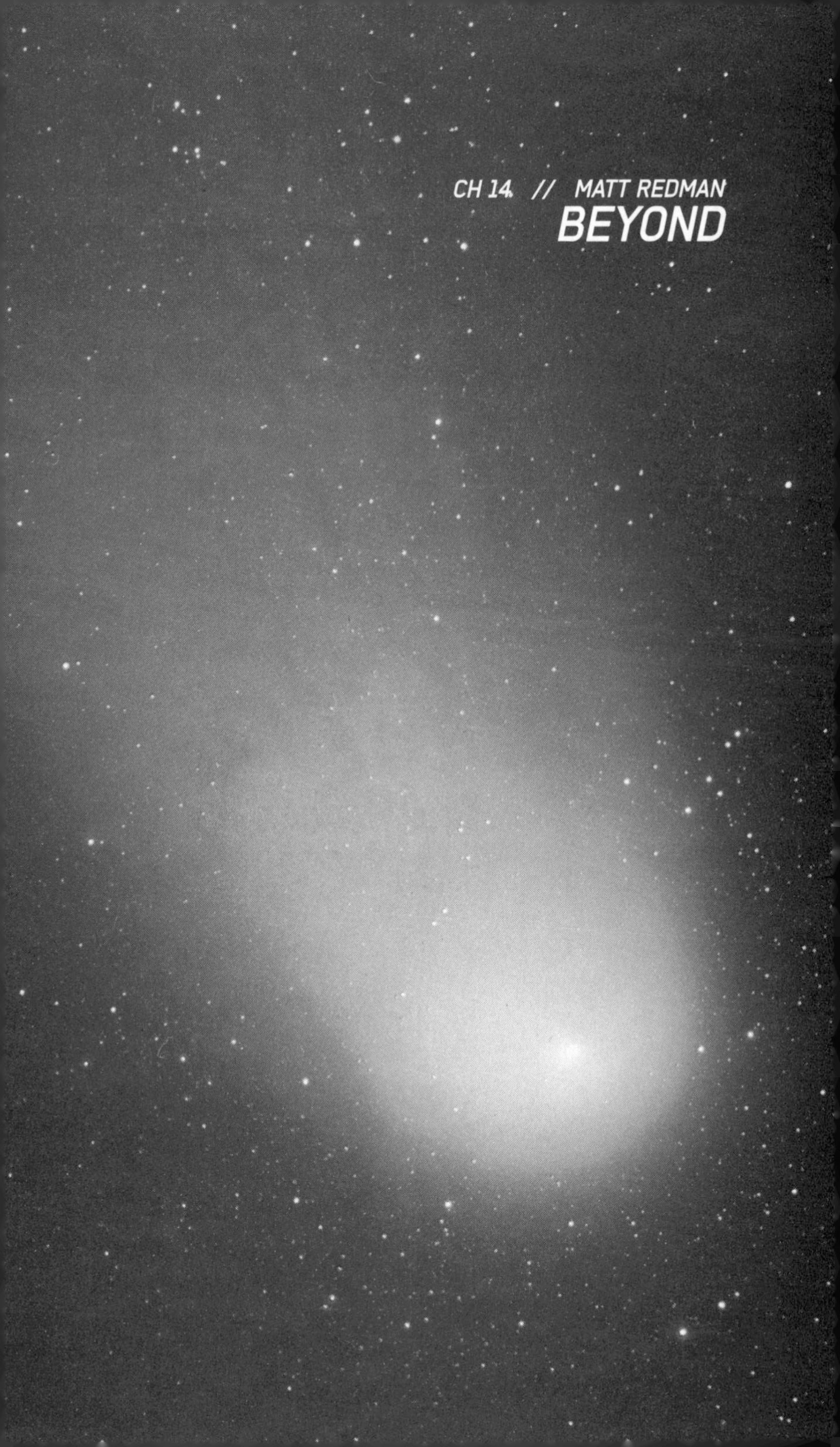

One Hundred Virgo Cluster Galaxies
These images taken by NASA's Hubble Space Telescope show the globular cluster systems of one
hundred galaxies observed within the Advanced Camera for Surveys (ACS) Virgo Cluster Survey.
Image and description: NASA, ESA, and E. Peng (Peking University, Beijing)

WE LIVE IN A UNIQUE AGE.

The introduction of air travel has created a global village—and these days practically every corner of Earth is within easy reach. Meanwhile, the Internet ushers in a generation of the familiar—with search engines placing a world of information at our fingertips. At the same time, video chats, social media, and email make friends thousands of miles across the globe seem as though they're only moments away.

Yet while the world has grown seemingly *smaller* to us, the universe, it seems, has grown *bigger*. Our telescopes remind us we're still only paddling in the shallows of an unfathomably large cosmos. And such a realization can only be healthy for the soul. For now and again, it's good for us to be confronted with things that are quite simply *out of reach*.

As we have already noted, even the closest stars are way beyond our grasp. The nearest of them, apart from the Sun, is Proxima Centauri. Scientists think this star is around 4.3 light-years away from us.[1] That being the case, you'd have to travel at 186,000 miles per second nonstop for over 4 years to reach it. Or, traveling by Concorde you would arrive in just over 2 million years. Let's not rush past these figures. In an age of the instant and the familiar, it can be so good to stretch our imaginations and dwell on some of these immense distances. Let's stick with Proxima Centauri for a moment and find a more pictorial explanation of exactly what it is we're encountering here. Say we have a ballpoint pen, and for the purposes of this illustration we imagine the tiny tip of that pen to be Earth. We place this pen on the ground, and then about 15 feet away we place a ping-pong ball, which on this scale represents our Sun. Sticking to this scale, how far away do we suppose we need to place a second ping-pong ball to represent Proxima Centauri? The answer is quite overwhelming. You would need to travel approximately 1,430 miles away to place that second ball. And, remember, except for the Sun, that's our nearest star neighbor.[2]

Looking beyond Proxima Centauri, scientists tell us that the stars on the far side of our Milky Way are perhaps twenty thousand times farther away than this. Our nearest neighboring spiral galaxy, Andromeda (the farthest object the unaided human eye can see), is said to be about twenty-five times farther away still. What's more, scientists believe the most-distant galaxies to be around three thousand times farther away from us than Andromeda is.[3] You may have lost grasp of the escalating numbers by now, but to put it bluntly, the universe is an outrageously big place to live. And for the most part, it's way, way out of our reach.

As huge and impressive as stars are, they are a mere dot on the cosmic landscape. Scientists estimate the average distance between them to be around twenty trillion miles.[4] As one astronomer describes it, "Place three grains of sand inside a vast cathedral, and the cathedral will be more closely packed with sand than space is with stars."[5]

In Psalm 90:4, the writer tells us that "a thousand years in [God's] sight are like a day that is just gone by." We know that not to be a mathematical statement, as the very same Scripture tells us those years are also like "a watch in the night"—or as another translation words it, "as brief as a few night hours" (NLT). The psalmist has stepped outside of the mathematical because he knows he cannot compute or weigh the awesomeness of God. Instead he dives into the poetic, shaping his words to try and somehow convey something of the nature of an eternal God who is Lord of all the years. He is reminding us that God's view of time is very different from ours. What we perceive as a huge stretch of time to Him is like just the tiniest of breaths.

And when we start to look at these vast perceived distances in the stretches of the universe, the very same rule applies. To us, these epic expanses are so hard to get our finite little minds around. To God Almighty, these distances are just a walk in the park. All that's completely out of reach to us is utterly accessible to Him, and held within His ever-capable hands. We cannot even begin to grasp the far reaches of this indescribable universe. How much less, then, can we claim to fathom the awesome Maker behind it all?

It's into this vast cosmic wilderness that humanity longs to probe. I'm writing this on the day the aptly named space shuttle *Discovery* returned home after a successful summer mission. Having traveled 5.8 million miles at speeds of around 17,000 miles per hour, it orbited Earth 219 times and then landed safely back home.[6] It was

another exciting day in the age of manned space exploration. But what is it within us that drives us to a mission like this? Is it a quest for power and knowledge, perhaps? Or just mere curiosity? Is it the hunt for other forms of life? Or are we driven simply by a desire to discover unknown resources? All of these factors no doubt play a part, and it's likely a mixture of all these motivations.

Maybe there is another reason for our desire to look through our telescopes and explore with our space shuttles. Perhaps it is something deep, deep down in the soul of humanity. Michael Collins, a former Gemini and Apollo astronaut, wrote, "It's human nature to stretch, to go, to see, to understand."[7] Could it be that our desire to explore the reaches of the universe is a God-given desire He Himself birthed in us? Might this longing to discover the heights and depths of creation stem from an underlying thirst to know Him, the Creator of it all? Is it just possible that our quest to search out something so much greater than ourselves is actually the heart cry of those who realize they are incomplete in and of themselves?

We surge upward in our spacecraft and gaze upward with our telescopes because we were made for something more. For every heart with the grace to recognize it, we soon find ourselves encountering the glory of God in the beauty of the universe.

MR

Nebula in Scorpius
Two stars orbit one another in the core of the large emission nebula NGC 6357 in Scorpius, about eight thousand light-years away from Earth.
Image and description: NASA, ESA, J. Maíz Apellániz (Instituto de Astrofísica de Andalucía, Spain), and STScI

NOTES:

1. NASA High Energy Astrophysics Science Archive Research Center, "The Nearest Star," heasarc.nasa.gov/docs/cosmic/nearest_star_info.html.

2. Illustration from *Astrosurf-Magazine,* www.astrosurf.com/benschop/Scale.htm.

3. T. Padmanabhan, "Ripples in the Early Universe," *Physics Education,* January–March 2007, 227.

4. NASA, "Educational Brief: Exploring the Interstellar Medium," cse.ssl.berkeley.edu/chips_epo/EducationBrief/CHIPS-Educational_Brief.htm.

5. James Jeans, quoted in Mark A. Garlick, *The Expanding Universe,* ed. John Gribbin (London: Dorling Kindersley, 2002), 7.

6. NASA Live Landing Coverage, August 9, 2005, www.nasa.gov/returntoflight/launch/landing-vlcc.html.

7. "Michael Collins," New Mexico Museum of Space History, www.nmspacemuseum.org/halloffame/detail.php?id=37.

THE UNIVERSE BEGINS TO LOOK MORE LIKE A GREAT THOUGHT THAN A GREAT MACHINE.

—JAMES JEANS
PHYSICIST AND ASTRONOMER

Helix Nebula

Located only 690 light-years from Earth, the Helix Nebula is one of our closest planetary nebula neighbors. Although the Helix Nebula looks simple, recent evidence has led astronomers to believe there might be a secondary doughnut lying perpendicular to the circular image seen here, possibly caused by a companion star at its core.

Image and description: NASA, ESA, C. R. O'Dell (Vanderbilt University), M. Meixner, and P. McCullough

CH 15 // LOUIE GIGLIO
INSIGHT

HIGH ABOVE THE RESORT-DOTTED KOHALA COAST, AND LURKING OVER THE LAVA-PAVED LANDSCAPE THAT composes much of the big island of Hawaii, one of Earth's premier vantage points is crawling with space lookers night after night. Standing at 13,600 feet (4,145 meters), high beyond the cloud line that often shrouds the dormant Mauna Kea volcano, the twin Keck telescopes provide "good seeing" almost every night of the year.

For astronomers, those earnest seekers of what lies beyond in the skies above, the words *good seeing* bode well. Yet the search for good seeing also drives them to remote and barren places, like the Atacama Desert in Chile—where the four-telescope array of the Very Large Telescope (or VLT—yes, that's what scientists named it) operates as part of the European Southern Observatory.

For the creators of these newer instruments like the Keck and the VLT, as well as early pioneers of the telescope like Lippershey, Janssen, Metius, Galileo, Kepler, and Newton, man's fascination with looking deeper into the universe has met with an ironic challenge.

While scientists believe that, as Earth dwellers, we inhabit one of the best platforms from which to observe space[1] (many factors contribute to our ability to see and understand more of space than we would from other vantage points in the cosmos), one of the components that allows us "good seeing" also hampers our view: namely, our own atmosphere. This unique, life-supporting band of wonder that makes our very existence possible also distorts our view of the heavens and at times clouds out the view altogether.

Science writer and historian Robert Zimmerman describes the predicament: "Dependant as we humans are on our eyesight, the atmosphere essentially left the human race blind to the heavens. We were like a nearsighted man before the invention of eyeglasses. We could squint and strain and maybe make a guess at what we were looking at, but to actually perceive the reality of the universe in all its glory was nigh on impossible."[2]

For decades, those thinking outside the scope of their current technological limitations dreamed of a space-based telescope with a view unimpaired by atmospheric conditions. In 1946, one of the fathers of this movement, Lyman Spitzer, wrote that such a project would perhaps "modify profoundly our basic concepts of space and time."[3]

As it turns out, Spitzer's assertion was right on the money.

What Spitzer and others envisioned was the stuff of sci-fi dreams, but it became reality in 1990 when NASA launched what, at the time, was Earth's third largest telescope into orbit.

Originally named LST, the Hubble Space Telescope weighed 24,500 pounds (11,110 kilograms), and hitched a ride on space shuttle *Discovery*. It took its place orbiting Earth at 353 miles (569 kilometers) above Earth's surface. Named after American astronomer

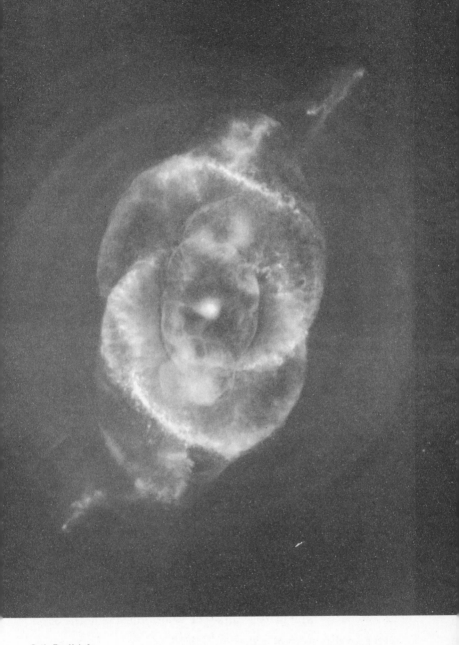

Cat's Eye Nebula
One of the most complex planetary nebulae ever seen in space, the Cat's Eye Nebula is shown here
in an image taken by the Hubble's Advanced Camera for Surveys. The rings around this nebula
are most likely caused by ejections of the central star's gaseous layers occurring at 1,500-year
intervals. What baffles astronomers is that the pattern drastically changed about 1,000 years ago,
resulting in the colorful fireworks display seen in the center of the nebula.

Image: X-ray: NASA/CXC/SAO; Optical: NASA/STScI

Edwin Hubble (1889–1953), Hubble circles the globe every 97 minutes.[4] It staked out a vantage point that would quickly revolutionize space observation and study.

Since Hubble's launch, writes Zimmerman, its "outpouring of spectacular images [including many within these pages] has been breathtaking and continuous. And with each new image the public has been given a better view of its place in the universe."[5]

Though revolutionary, in time the achievement of the HST will be surpassed by greater attempts to see and understand more of the universe. Aided by advancements in technology and scientific discovery, we will continue to build bigger and more impressive Earth- and space-based telescopes (such as the James Webb Space Telescope) in our quest to see farther than ever before.

Yet for all our straining to see what God has made, He will never have to so much as squint to see you and me. Though high above the heavens, and capable of measuring the entirety of space with the breadth of His fingers, God has no trouble seeing you, His prized creation and most loved possession.

The psalmist wrote, "By the word of the LORD were the heavens made, their starry host by the breath of his mouth" (33:6). But just when we might be tempted to believe that God is too big to be concerned with someone as tiny as you or me, we read, "From heaven the LORD looks down and sees all mankind; from his dwelling place he watches all who live on earth—he who forms the hearts of all, who considers everything they do" (33:13–15).

It's overwhelming (and somewhat dehumanizing) to realize that there are close to seven billion of us alive on the planet at this moment. But before we think it's too much for God to know everything about every single one of us, we have to remember that there are more stars than that in just *one arm* of the Milky Way Galaxy.[6] In fact, the Milky Way contains hundreds of billions of stars, and our God put each one in its place.

"He who brings out the starry host one by one, and calls them each by name. Because of his great power and mighty strength, not one of them is missing" (Isa. 40:26). It's crazy to think that God can name each of the stars. But what's more stunning is that He can call you by your name as well.

God is big, but He's not too big to miss you in the crowd.

In this massive ocean of cosmic dark, you are not alone, or unnoticed. He knows the exact number of hairs on your head, and the number of fears in your heart. With God, it's always "good seeing." In the brightness of day or shrouded night, His eyes never lose sight of you. Whether you feel as though you're a long way off, or even if you can sense that He is near, God is closer than your very next breath.

God doesn't need a Hubble Telescope to get in touch with you or check on the affairs of your life. He sees it all, the good and the bad, the joy and the pain. But not only does God see, He has the power to heal and repair, to carry and to hold.

He sees your fears—so why not bring them to Him?

He sees your wrongs—so why not confess them and receive His grace and forgiveness?

He sees your struggles—so why not stop pretending and lean on Jesus for strength?

He sees your questions and doubts—so be honest with Him.

He sees your dreams and aspirations—so put them in His hands.

THE LARGER THE ISLAND OF KNOWLEDGE, THE LONGER THE SHORELINE OF WONDER.

—RALPH W. SOCKMAN

He sees your motives and intentions—so let Him work beneath the surface.

He sees your deepest needs—He alone can meet them.

God knows everything that's true about you, and He loves you anyway. You are His offspring, His creation, His idea.

And you were made to know and love Him deeply, reflecting His great glory like the stars.

LG

Take a moment now to read and reflect on Psalm 139:1-14:

O LORD, you have searched me and you know me. You know when I sit and when I rise; you perceive my thoughts from afar. You discern my going out and my lying down; you are familiar with all my ways. Before a word is on my tongue you know it completely, O LORD. You hem me in—behind and before; you have laid your hand upon me. Such knowledge is too wonderful for me, too lofty for me to attain. Where can I go from your Spirit? Where can I flee from your presence? If I go up to the heavens, you are there; if I make my bed in the depths, you are there. If I rise on the wings of the dawn, if I settle on the far side of the sea, even there your hand will guide me, your right hand will hold me fast. If I say, "Surely the darkness will hide me and the light become night around me," even the darkness will not

be dark to you; the night will shine like the day, for
darkness is as light to you. For you created my inmost
being; you knit me together in my mother's womb.
I praise you because I am fearfully and wonderfully
made; your works are wonderful, I know that full
well.

NOTES:

1. Guillermo Gonzalez and Jay Wesley Richards, *The Privileged Planet: How Our Place in the Universe Is Designed for Discovery* (Washington, DC: Regnery, 2004), 101.

2. Robert Zimmerman, *The Universe in a Mirror* (Princeton, NJ: Princeton University Press, 2007), 7.

3. Lyman Spitzer, quoted in Carolyn Collins Petersen and John C. Brandt, *Hubble Vision: Further Adventures with the Hubble Space Telescope* (Cambridge, UK: Cambridge University Press, 1998), 195.

4. HubbleSite, "Hubble Essentials: Quick Facts," hubblesite.org/the_telescope/hubble_essentials/quick_facts.php.

5. Zimmerman, 180.

6. NASA, "Two of the Milky Way's Spiral Arms Go Missing," June 2, 2008, www.nasa.gov/mission_pages/spitzer/news/spitzer-20080603-10am.html.

ABOUT LOUIE GIGLIO AND MATT REDMAN

■ **Louie Giglio** is the pastor of Passion City Church in Atlanta, Georgia, and the founder of the Passion Movement. From its start in 1995, Passion has sought to inspire the university-aged generation to live for the name and renown of Jesus. Hosting gatherings in cities around the globe, Passion continues to be a catalyst for awakening, justice, and worship that ripple far beyond Passion events.

Louie is also a speaker and author, whose books include *The Air I Breathe—Worship as a Way of Life* and *i am not but i know I AM*. His DVD messages, *Indescribable* and *How Great Is Our God*, have been seen by millions of people worldwide. He and his wife, Shelley, are founders of sixstepsrecords, a family of artist-worshippers whose music reflects the Passion journey.

■ **Matt Redman** is a songwriter and worship leader based in Brighton, England. His songs, including *Blessed Be Your Name*, *The Heart of Worship*, *You Never Let Go*, and *Our God*, have influenced the worship vocabulary of the global church. As an author, Matt has written several books on worship, including *The Unquenchable Worshipper*, *Facedown,* and *Mirror Ball.*

Since 2000, Matt has worked alongside Louie and Shelley as a vital part of the Passion Movement, including two years in Atlanta with his family for the beginnings of Passion City Church. Matt is married to Beth, and they have five children.

Matt (Left) and Louie (Right)
Image: Lee Steffen

ACKNOWLEDGMENTS

The writing of this book has been an inspiring journey. We're so grateful to all who have contributed their expertise and encouragement along the way:

Dr. Jennifer Wiseman, currently the Senior Project Scientist for NASA's Hubble Space Telescope. Former and current astronauts Joe Tanner, Mike Good, Pat Forrester, and Shane Kimbrough. Thanks also to Matt Walden.

Jennifer Hill and Brad Jones, who carried a huge portion of the details and logistics and kept the project moving in the midst of everything else going on in our world. Special thanks to Eddie Kirkland, a vital part of this book in its early stages and the person responsible for computing the oft-repeated size comparisons in the *Indescribable* and *How Great Is Our God* messages. (If Earth were a golf ball ...)

Partners Alex Field, Don Pape, and the team at David C Cook, who believed in this book and the value of bringing an image-rich book to people.

Chris Tomlin for inviting us to be a part of two amazing tours that gave us the opportunity to carry the content of these pages to the world.

And most especially to our wives, Shelley Giglio and Beth Redman.

SELECTED BIBLIOGRAPHY

Listed below is source information for the call-out quotes that appear throughout the book. Please see the end of each chapter for additional references.

Addison, Joseph. "Ode." *Poets' Corner.*
theotherpages.org/poems/addison1.html.

Augustine. *City of God,* XI, 4, 2. In *Basic Writings of St. Augustine.*
Edited by W. J. Oates. New York: Random House, 1948.

Collins, Francis. "Why This Scientist Believes in God." *CNN.*
(April 6, 2007.) www.cnn.com/2007/US/04/03/collins.commentary/index.html.

De Fontenelle, Bernard. Quoted in Edward Robert Harrison. *Masks of the Universe: Changing Ideas on the Nature of the Cosmos.* 2nd ed. New York: Cambridge University Press, 2003. Page 101.

Emerson, Ralph Waldo. "Nature." In *Essays and Lectures.* New York: Literary Classics, 1983. Page 9.

Jeans, James. Quoted in Elizabeth Leane. *Reading Popular Physics: Disciplinary Skirmishes and Textual Strategies.* Burlington, VT: Ashgate, 2007. Page 31.

Kendrick, Graham. "From Heaven You Came." Quoted in William J. Petersen and Ardythe Petersen. *The Complete Book of Hymns: Inspiring Stories about 600 Hymns and Praise Songs.* Carol Stream, IL: Tyndale, 2006. Page 217.

Mitchell, Edgar. Quoted in Kevin W. Kelley, ed. *The Home Planet.* Reading, MA: Addison-Wesley, 1988. Page 43.

Phillpotts, Eden. *A Shadow Passes.* Macmillan, 1934.

Plato. *The Dialogues of Plato.* Translated by B. Jowett. London: Macmillan, 1871. Page 364.

Prigogine, Ilya, Gregoire Nicolis, and Agnes Babloyantz. "Thermodynamics of Evolution." *Physics Today* 25, no. 11 (1972). Pages 23–28.

Schaefer, Henry F. *Science and Christianity: Conflict or Coherence?*
    Athens, GA: Apollos Trust, 2004. Page 42.

Sockman, Ralph W. Quoted in Donald D. Hoffman. *Visual
    Intelligence: How We Create What We See.* New York: Norton,
    1998. Page xiii.

Van Dyke, Henry. "Joyful, Joyful We Adore Thee." (1907.) *Cyber
    Hymnal.* www.cyberhymnal.org/htm/j/o/joyful.htm.

A DVD TALK BY **LOUIE GIGLIO**

THE MESSAGE
SEEN AND SHARED
BY MILLIONS
AROUND THE WORLD

Join Louie Giglio as *Indescribable* takes us on an image-rich journey through the cosmos, allowing us to peer into God's universe to discover the amazing magnitude of His greatness and grace.